Sins Of A Queen

Italian Appetizers and Desserts

Valentina Cirasola

To Denise,
Enjoy my books
again and again—
Love,

Outskirts Press, Inc.
Denver, Colorado

Sins Of A Queen
Italian Appetizers and Desserts
All Rights Reserved.
Copyright © 2011 Valentina Cirasola
V5.0

Outskirts Press, Inc.
http://www.outskirtspress.com

ISBN: 978-1-4327-6206-3

Outskirts Press and the "OP" logo are trademarks belonging to Outskirts Press, Inc.

PRINTED IN THE UNITED STATES OF AMERICA

Dedicated To My Mother
the designer of me

The day you left this world, a new light came on in the heart of the galaxy.
Your love that once embraced me is now vibrating around me and
it fills up the emptiness of my spirit.
Live on, mamma!

♥

Table of Contents

Salt is the spice of food, attitude is the spice of life

Right now, you might be asking yourself why a successful interior designer writes about food. It is only about attitude. Getting up in the morning and being able to do what I love is a success. My first concern, when I get up in the morning is to prepare my few cups of espresso coffee with breakfast Italian style, while I am reading a book, a classic music playing in the background and a scented candle creating my atmosphere. I ease into the day instead of rushing in it. Espresso runs in my veins instead of blood. **Espresso coffee is my first sin.**

My food is planned early in the morning, after the breakfast ritual. I think about what I am going to eat for dinner and plan for it at the beginning of the day, that means going to the market between clients' appointments and my office work. My lunch is also planned in the early morning, if I will not spend it with clients or friends, otherwise it is the social part of my working day. I like to break breads with people while we are conducting business, just as Romans met with their business associates and made business deals laying down on triclinium while eating for long hours. **Bread is my second sin.**

We Italian have a passion for fast cars, fast thinking, quick actions, snappy temper, hot and vivid colours, but we love, love, love slow food. Women in Italy dress up just to go to the near by street food market. They must look good as the attractive food they will put on the table for the family. Being Italian born and have lived all my life in Italy, I have acquired the same fast thinking and brought it along with me anywhere I lived in the world. Today, living in California, I teach the same love for food, spreading lightheartedness and joy, while passing my notions of good life and health through good eating.

Italian food is not only about pizzas and pasta dishes loaded with cheese. Oh, by the way, Italians never overdose on cheese. Cheese is supposed to be one of the many elements of a condiment and it is not supposed to shadow other ingredients and overpowering the taste. Let's say, we are preparing a "Pizza Quattro Stagioni" (four seasons pizza), we want to taste the ripe tomatoes and mozzarella, prosciutto and artichokes conserved in olive oil, anchovies and capers, fresh mushrooms, finally the basil leaves and the "green gold" as we call our local olive oil. The flavour of each ingredient must come through distinctively and in one single file, the bread of the pizza must reunite them all in its crunchiness and flavour. **Cheese is my third sin.**

Italian food specialties include lot of weekly and in some areas daily fresh fish, as in Bari, my hometown. Fish must be live, moving and kicking when we bring it home, or at least freshly caught in the small hours of the night and brought in the port at dawn. It is very common, in the early morning to see the fisherman banks filled with a crowd of people choosing the catch of the day and talking to each other about recipes and ways to prepare some of the fish. A small piece of advice: when ordering fish in restaurants, don't feel bad to send back to the kitchen a stinking fish. Fresh fish whether is from the sea, ocean or fresh water, never smells bad. Since I was a baby, I have had an incredible love for raw fish and the best time eating it. **Fish is my fourth sin.**

During summer, to fight the outrageous heat, we indulge in gelato delights. Only in Italy people go out in the afternoon for a daily "passeggiata", the Italian leisurely stroll in downtown elegant areas, while looking at fashionable windows, or along the sea promenade. Parks are also good places to stroll while licking a gelato. Otherwise sweets are mostly reserved for Sunday dinners or special occasions. Lunches and dinners in Italy always end with fresh fruit. **Fruit is my fifth sin.**

Desserts made of fruits are very common in Italy. The sugar exuding from the fruits is the natural sweetener and the enhancement could be either honey or any aromatic liquor, especially those based on orange flavours. Chocolate biscotti and dark chocolates in all forms and shapes, chipped, shaved, fluffed up, dusted on, made into ribbons, or ganache covers are the highlight in "small quantity" of our fruit desserts. Italians do indulgence but with moderation.

Chocolate becomes divine when is paired up with special red wines, or Muscat of which Italy produces so many excellent qualities, or even with Prosecco and classic Champagne. Try dark chocolate with a light-bodied wine. Absolutely a yes, when it is a Pinot Noir with a light tart raspberry notes in the Pinot to be matched with a fruity bitterness of the dark chocolate. The other match I like is a Merlot medium body with a cherry note to be matched with the tart dried cherries in the bittersweet chocolate.

As clumsy as it sounds perfection is perfect, why mess with it. **Chocolate and wines are my sixth sin.**

I learned in my early age to love salt. I offer a few laughs in the chapter of my Baptism Ceremony. Salt in history was regarded as a precious item. Romans' salary was paid with salt, hence the origin of the word salary, from "salario". In the Italian language there is even a way to describe a high price product: "salato" meaning a product has been salted (in the price) to a high level that only the elite can afford to touch it.

Salt is the main spice of food. It is necessary as much as are all other elements of food. Our body needs unconditionally everything, from pasta, rice and breads, to sugar, salt and fat; from protein to minerals; from vegetables to fruits, nuts and wines, exactly all the elements any diet denies. The secret in staying healthy is not to follow all the possible diets invented. The secret is to eat everything without restriction, but in small portions and more times during the day.

One good practice to keep a balanced weight forever is to keep in the garderobe one pair of pants, it doesn't matter if it is out of fashion, it is only needed for measurements. The goal is to keep fitting in that one pair of pants for many years. We should wear it once every month, if it doesn't fit, it is time to reduce the food portions for a couple of months. By doing this, we are in control of our food and not food in control of us. **Salt is my seventh sin.**

Spice up food and spice up life, create a great attitude around food. Food is not our enemy, but fuel for the brain. Food consumed in moderation and without deprivation will maintain our beauty and our inner harmony.

There's a red-hot passion for the best things in life that runs in my Italian culture. Why put a limitation to passions? Writing about food and designing kitchens, or wine cellars, those rooms that have a "make me feel good" tag attached, is one of the many things I enjoy doing. Decorating dining tables to host colourful food for the enjoyment of guests is a pleasure. There is no other reason why I indulge in writing about food, other than leaving behind a trail of my knowledge. Bari my hometown in the region of Puglia in Italy now has its own Queen!

The day of the baptism ceremony

I was born in Bari, the largest city in the southern region of Puglia, in Italy.

At the time of my birth, Italy was predominantly Catholic. Newborn babies in Italy received the sacrament of Baptism within a couple of months of their birth and still do.

It is the first step to introduce a baby into a "civilized" world. The ceremony of Baptism has always been a big, important feast for an Italian family then and now.

The baby, boy or girl indifferently, is dressed in the first white dress. Guests wear the latest fashion and bring expensive gift to the parents, mostly gold items that baby will keep for life as investment. A formal ceremony is booked with the church and a formal reception is also booked with a restaurant to celebrate the event, which becomes an opportunity to thank everybody for his or her generosity.

My parents had a difficult time to get me baptized in the first two months of my life, times were tough then, but they did the best with what they had. My turn to be baptized came when I was already nine months old, talking and walking.

We went to the church with only a few aunts and no other guests and I walked like a toddler down the nave, touching everything, curious of my surroundings, talking and laughing out loud. I had no concept of a church yet.

In front of us, there was another Baptism ceremony taking place, I guess we were early for my event. We set and waited our turn, but I was a curious baby. My parents and my aunts started conversing quietly and I took advantage of their momentarily distraction to sneak out of their control and roam around the church.

When my turn to be seen by the priest arrived, I was no were to be found. My parents, my aunts, the priest and his church helpers all went searching for me, the "terrible" toddler, who might had gone out of the church into the street. I was finally found on the altar, singing, drinking the wine in the Holy Chalice and playing with the candleholders.

Wow! My father was furious when they all realized where I was.

It took a whole lot to get me down, but I was taken down the altar against my desire, of course, screaming, crying and kicking and finally they got me baptized. The scene was comical and not a traditional scene, where you see the father and mother holding the newborn baby in their arms, the priest administering the sacrament of the Baptism with Holy Water and the guests around participating to the ceremony with their prayers.

I was a walking chubby baby, I liked to eat since then, the only thing they could do was to keep me firmly planted on the floor. I really liked receiving the Holy Water, it was salty and tasty. I asked for some more, the priest told me to shut up and be quiet. I asked for some more, the priest told me to shut up and be quiet, but I wanted some more salty water. Now, you can imagine the rest of the event and the embarrassment of my parents. By screaming, crying and kicking, I got what I wanted, got blessed a few more times than necessary and my love for savoury, salty food started in that moment.

My Mom told me this story a few times in my life; her recollection of this event was so much funnier than the way I can ever tell the story. She lived it in first person and I am telling you, it was funny to hear it from her.

Orecchiette Pasta Farm Style
Duration: 25 min.

Ingredients for 4 people
1 lb. of orecchiette pasta (whole wheat OK) or any short pasta as rotini
grated Parmigiano cheese
3 oz. of ricotta salata (salty ricotta), or feta cheese
1 pack of red cherry tomatoes cubed
1 pack of red small pear yellow tomatoes cubed
3 cloves of chopped garlic
a hand full of basil leaves, oregano and Italian parsley
salt and black pepper to taste
extra-virgin olive oil
a hand full of breadcrumbs

Wash and chop all the ingredients, place them in a large mixing bowl, except breadcrumbs to be added last.

Macerate all the ingredients together to marry the flavours for at least 30 minutes. The ingredients will be raw.

In a pot bring salted water to a boil.

Cook the pasta very "**al dente**". Reserve 1 cup of the cooking water.

Drain the water. Add the hot pasta to the rest of the ingredients, one cup of cooking water, mix well and rest it for about five minutes to let the pasta get a little softer and the ingredients come together.

Add another hand full of Parmigiano cheese and a handful of breadcrumbs with a swirl of olive oil. Adjust seasoning.

This dish can be served in a decorative bowl, or in single ramekins.

Rotini Farm Style

Pearl Barley Salad With Arrucola
Duration: 35 min.

Ingredients for 4 people
2 oz. per person of pearl barley[1]
8 oz. of cooked chickpeas (canned OK)
3 or 4 bay leaves
1 bunch of arrucola
juice of ½ lemon
Parmigiano cheese
extra-virgin olive oil
salt and black pepper to your taste

In a pot full of salted water boil pearl barley and cook it **al dente**. To cook pasta, rice or any grain al dente means to leave it slightly hard when tested under the teeth.

In a separate pot cook the chickpeas slowly; better if using the slow cooker, or a pressure cooker. When cooking beans, add a few bay leaves in the water[2].

In a serving bowl mix together pearl barley and cooked chickpeas.

Add freshly squeezed lemon juice, salt and pepper and olive oil.

Toss well, check your seasoning - adjust salt, pepper & lemon to your taste.

Allow resting for 15 minutes.

Before serving add arrucola and Parmigiano cheese shaved in ribbons strips.

Mix and serve at room temperature, not cold directly from the refrigerator.

Note
1. Pearl barley is a medieval grain mostly used by the workers and low-income people to keep a full stomach and do hard work for long hours.
2. All beans contain oligosaccharide sugar that the human body cannot process. The lining of the small intestine cannot break down and absorb the large molecule of oligosaccharides, because the body does not produce the enzyme that breaks them down. Many people have problems when eating beans. Adding bay leaves to the beans during cooking helps the digestion immensely.

Shrimps Piquant In Rice Ring
Duration: 35 min.

Ingredients for 4 people

2 lb. of uncooked shrimps
2 green bell peppers
2 or 3 stalks of celery
1 onion
3 or 4 peeled tomatoes
1 or 2 tablespoons of tomato sauce
1 egg beaten

3 laurel leaves (bay leaves OK)
a hand full of thyme
a few lemon slices
olive oil and truffle oil
butter to grease a baking pan
cayenne pepper, salt to your liking
grated Parmigiano cheese

Wash all vegetables, deseed bell peppers and cut everything in the same size.

Sauté all the vegetables in olive oil until translucent. Add chopped peeled tomatoes, tomato sauce and all the spices. Cook for about ten minutes, add the shrimps skin off.

Continue to simmer at low fire for about ten more minutes. Adjust seasoning to taste.

Aside cook the rice, as it is most convenient to you. Italians boil rice in salted boiling water as we do for pasta and then we drain the water. Butter a baking pan with a hole in the centre, mostly used for cakes and Charlottes, better if it has a collapsible bottom.

In the rice mix one egg and some grated Parmigiano cheese.

Place all the cooked rice in the baking pan with a few dollops of butter on top, press well and bake at 400° F until the top is golden.

Turn the baked rice over a serving plate, inside of the centre hole arrange the shrimps, sauce and all the ingredients. Add a swirl of truffle oil over the rice.

Shrimps Piquant In Rice Ring

Garlic Flavoured Cheese On Celery
Duration: 15 min.

Ingredients for 4 people

1 celery stalk per person
4 garlic cloves
7 oz. of any cream cheese,
  or plain chêvre cheese

2 cans of anchovy fillets in olive oil
salt and black pepper to taste

Divide each stalk of celery, wash the dirt in between stalks; with a potato peeler take out the thin layer of fibre strings from the backside of the stalks.

Cut each stalk in small bites of about 3".

Reserve in the refrigerator until the cream is prepared.

In the food processor mix all the ingredients and only 1 can of anchovies, until a smooth cream is formed.

Fill each celery stalk with this savoury cream and add one piece of anchovies on each celery stalk as decorative touch. Serve chilled. It is refreshing and tasty.

—m—

Radishes Filled With Hot Cheese
Duration: 15 min.

Ingredients for 4 people

various pieces of left over cheese
½ cup dry white wine

1 or 2 cloves of garlic
black pepper to your taste, only if cheeses are bland

Put together all the left over pieces of various cheeses that you have in the refrigerator, place them in a food processor. Add 1 or 2 cloves of garlic, ½ cup of dry white wine and blend thoroughly until creamy.

Wash the radishes, cut the leaves off and cut both ends off. Make a cross cut on the base of the radishes. With a spreading knife, fill the centre of each radish with a formaggio forte (hot cheese) and make a small hill on top. To serve, place them on a bed of rock salt to prevent from moving around once they have been filled.

Use this hot cheese any way you like to fill the radishes, or to fill cherry tomatoes, or to spread on toasted bread, or even to serve with raw celery as a dip.

Parsley Zucchini
Duration: 20 min.

Ingredients for 4 people
4 Italian zucchini
American bread sliced
butter or margarine
a hand full of Italian parsley
3 or 4 cloves of chopped garlic
grated Parmigiano cheese
extra-virgin olive oil
salt and black pepper to taste

Cut the crust from the American bread slices. Reserve the crust to make breadcrumbs at a different time.

Spread butter or margarine (room temperature) over each slice and place in the oven under the broiler to toast and brown both sides. When done cut each slice in triangles and place them on a serving dish.

Meanwhile, wash the zucchini and cut both ends off.

Split the zucchini in half. Cut a bit of the white spongy part off, then cut the zucchini in very thin strips the long way.

Parboil the zucchini strips for only 5 or 6 minutes in salted water; pat them dry in a cloth or absorbent paper.

Sprinkle raw chopped garlic and lot of chopped parsley on top of the toasted bread, then place the zucchini on top.

Drizzle extra-virgin olive oil, season with salt and pepper to your liking and finish them off with a light sprinkle of Parmigiano cheese.

Zucchini Stuffed With Carrot Mousse
Duration: 20 min.

Ingredients for 4 people
1 zucchini per person
1 carrot per person
1 whole egg
¼ cup of milk
1 garlic clove
grated Parmigiano cheese
a hand full of Italian parsley
extra-virgin olive oil
salt and black pepper to taste

Peel the carrots, chop coarsely and cook them in boiling salted water until very soft. In the food processor mix all the ingredients except the zucchini and olive oil. Make a smooth mousse, adjust the seasoning, mix well and set aside.

Wash the zucchini, cut both ends off, split them in half. With a teaspoon create a channel in the centre by taking out the white spongy part.

In a pan bring salted water to a boil. Drop the zucchini in the boiling water for only five minutes to parboil them, meaning to make them slightly cooked.

Oil a baking pan. Fill each zucchini half with carrot mousse.

Align them up in the baking pan, add a swirl of olive oil over, grated Parmigiano cheese, salt and black pepper to your taste and bake at 375° F until golden brown.

Zucchini Flowers Fritters
Duration: 50 min.

Ingredients for 4 people
1 lb. of zucchini flowers
6 oz. of white flour
2 beaten eggs
¼ of beer yeast cube, or 1 pack of dry yeast
a pinch of sugar
1 tablespoon of olive oil
water as needed
grated Parmigiano cheese
a hand full of chopped Italian parsley and chives
salt and black pepper to taste
vegetable oil for frying

Wash the zucchini flowers very well inside and outside. Often the centre of the zucchini flowers hosts ants and insects. Gently pat them dry. Leave the zucchini flowers whole.

Beat the eggs first. Make a dense batter by combining all the ingredients except the zucchini flowers and salt. While mixing the batter, add warm water in small quantity as needed.

Add beaten eggs, season to your taste. Mix gently. Cover the bowl with a plastic wrap. Let the batter rest away from wind drafts. The batter will rise and bubbles will form at the top. It should double in size. Incorporate the zucchini flowers in the batter.

In a frying skillet warm up the vegetable oil, then spoon by spoon, drop the puffy batter into the hot oil. Make each circle about 3" in diameter.

Fry until each fritter is golden brown and crispy. Drain the excess oil on absorbent paper. Season with salt and black pepper to taste.

To serve prepare a bed of colourful radicchio leaves for a good colour contrast, place the zucchini flower fritters on top, sprinkle chopped parsley and chives.

What a delicacy!

Baked Cherry Tomatoes
Duration: 30 min.

Ingredients for 4 people
1 lb. of fresh cherry tomatoes
extra-virgin olive oil
¼ cup of vegetable broth (water OK)
a hand full of fresh basil leaves
salt and pepper to taste

Wash the cherry tomatoes, poke a small hole in each one and place them in a baking dish, cover the cherry tomatoes half way with olive oil, salt and pepper.

To make a more consistent sauce, add ¼ cup of vegetable broth, or water if you like to have less calories.

Bake at 350° F. Tomatoes must be wrinkled and their own juice must exude, which mixed with the olive oil will create a delicate golden sauce.

At the end chop fresh basil leaves to add more colour and flavour to the tomatoes.

Eat these little baked tomatoes on top of crusty bread, with or without a slice of your favourite cheese, or as an accompaniment to a fish or meat plate.

They are God's jewels on earth!

Naples Style Bell Peppers Dance
Duration: 35 min.

Ingredients for 4 people
4 coloured bell peppers
1 onion finely sliced
5 peeled tomatoes
3 tablespoons of capers
5 to 6 tablespoons of olive oil
vegetable broth
a hand full of breadcrumbs
a hand full of Italian parsley
Pecorino cheese
salt, black pepper to taste

Wash the peppers, split them in half, take the seeds out and then cut small strips about ½ " wide.

In a frying pan sauté onion and all the bell peppers in olive oil.

Season with salt and black pepper to taste.

Cover the frying pan and cook for about 10 minutes at medium fire.

Add peeled tomatoes and ½ cup of vegetable stock. Continue the cooking for about 10-15 more minutes until the peppers are soft but not mushy and the sauce has thickened.

Finish the cooking with capers, finely chopped parsley and breadcrumbs. Breadcrumbs will add texture. Shave some Pecorino cheese over.

Serve this dish with a crunchy Pugliese style bread and a glass of rose' or red wine. It can be made into a specialty sandwich, with a soft cheese.

By adding pasta it can be turned into a main meal, or it can be used as a side vegetable for meat and fish.

Roasted Peppers

Roasted Peppers
Duration: 40 min.

Ingredients for 4 people

4 red and yellow bell peppers
4 teaspoons of capers
5 or 6 anchovies
a hand full of basil leaves
salt, black pepper to your taste

3 or 4 cloves of garlic finely chopped
½ cup of black-pitted olives, or Calamata Greek olives
a hand full of chopped Italian parsley
extra-virgin olive oil to your liking

Wash the peppers. Place the peppers whole on a cookie sheet and roast them in the oven at 375° F for about 30-40 minutes, or until scorched on all of the sides. Check them often, making sure not to burn them.

Place them on a plate and cover with a plastic film to retain the moisture and to cool them down.

Remove the plastic and peel the skin off as soon as they are manageable to the touch, take the seeds out and set them aside in a serving dish.

With your fingers (do not need a knife for the next operation) tear the pulp of the peppers into strips of about ¼ " wide. Do not drain the juice that will form.

Add the condiments: garlic finely chopped, capers, olives, anchovies cut in small pieces, parsley, basil leaves, salt, black pepper or hot pepper and olive oil.

Toss it gently. Serve it warm, or at room temperature. Do not chill it.

It is an excellent appetizer, or a nice accompaniment to meat or fish dishes, with a few slices of Pugliese bread, or sourdough bread.

—〰—

Lightly Fried Peppers
Duration: 20 min.

Ingredients for 4 people

Use five or six bell peppers in all three colours, red, yellow and red. Wash and take seeds out. Split them and cut strips of about 1-1/2" or 2" wide. In a skillet warm up ½ cup of vegetable oil and drop in all the strips of peppers. Let them brown on all sizes; season with salt and peppers to your liking when done.

Use them in sandwiches, or alone just like that.

Dandelions Salad
Duration: 30 min.

Ingredients for 4 people
2 bunches of dandelions
6 cherry tomatoes
6 Yukon gold potatoes
a hand full of piñoli (pine nuts) not toasted
wine vinegar
extra-virgin olive oil
salt, black pepper, or chili pepper to taste

Wash the skin of the potatoes; boil them with the skin on. Keep a firm consistency; do not overcook the potatoes, because they will be sliced later.

Drain the water out and peel the skin off as soon as the potatoes are manageable, but still warm. Cut them in circular slices about ½" thick.

Meanwhile clean and wash well the dandelions.

Cut them in small bite size pieces, also using the stems[1], which is the best part.

In a large serving bowl mix the raw dandelions and the boiled potatoes cut in slices.

Add olive oil and wine vinegar very generously. Don't use balsamic vinegar, it will stain the potatoes, you want to keep the colour of this salad very vividly. Continue with the rest of the ingredients, cherry tomatoes split in half, piñoli (pine nuts), season with salt and black pepper, or chili pepper to taste.

Mix it gently trying not to break the potatoes.

For this salad I use more condiment than usual, because the potatoes are porous and absorb most of the condiment.

Do not refrigerate it! Serve it either warm, or at room temperature.

Note

In the States, dandelions with the stems are hard to find. Evidently stems are considered not an eatable part, therefore they are cut away before the dandelions arrive to the supermarket.

Stuffed Baked Potatoes
Duration: 75 min.

Ingredients for 4 people

4 large potatoes
3 oz. of salami
3.5 oz. of Provolone or any sharp cheese
4 eggs
1 onion

a few dollops of butter
olive oil
cooking oil spray
salt and pepper to your liking

Wrap each potato in aluminium foil; place them in the oven at 400° F. for about an hour. Take the potatoes out of foil and let them cool down.

Carefully and making sure the potatoes remain whole, spoon out the centre to create a groove in the middle so it can be filled with ingredients. Reserve the potatoes pulp scooped out from the centre.

Cube onion, Provolone cheese and salami all in the same size. Beat the eggs.

In a skillet sauté onion in olive oil, add reserved potatoes pulp, salami and cheese. Let the flavours come together. Add beaten eggs.

Season with salt and black pepper to your liking. Mix well until all the ingredients are amalgamated.

Fill the centre of the baked potatoes with this mixture.

Lightly spray a baking pan with cooking oil, align the filled potatoes, lightly sprinkle the top with grated Pecorino cheese, add a few dollops of butter on top of each potatoes and bake until they are golden brown.

Grilled Asparagus

Grilled Asparagus
Duration: 30 min.

Ingredients for 4 people
2 bunches of asparagus
3 eggs
breadcrumbs
extra-virgin olive oil
juice of ½ lemon
salt and black pepper to taste

Peel the asparagus the long way with a potato peeler to remove the first layer of hard skin. Leave the tips on.

Roll them in olive oil and salt, grill them either in a grill pan on the stove, or directly on the outdoor grill, as it is most convenient to you.

Make grill marks, will look good when serving.

Aside hard-boil the eggs. Peel the shells when manageable, slice the eggs with egg slicer, or crumble them.

Place the asparagus on a serving dish; add sliced hard-boiled eggs bunched up only at the end of the asparagus.

Lightly sprinkle breadcrumbs and season with salt and pepper to your liking.

Prepare a small citronette with olive oil, fresh lemon juice and salt and pepper.

Drizzle it over the whole composition.

Salad Of Tomatoes Variety

Salad Of Tomatoes Variety
Duration: 15 min.

Ingredients for 4 people
green zebra tomatoes
yellow pear tomatoes
red pear tomatoes
cherry tomatoes
2 shallots
8 Mozzarella bocconcini[1]
2 oz. of black olives
sherry vinegar, or roasted apple vinegar
4 or 5 garlic cloves and salt to make a paste
extra-virgin olive oil
salt and black pepper to taste

Finely chop the shallots. Leave it to macerate in a sherry vinegar, or roasted apple vinegar.

To make a garlic paste:
On a wooden board chop the garlic cloves, add salt and with the blade of the knife scrape the garlic against the wooden board, continue to chop and scrape the garlic until it becomes creamy. Reserve. It will be used in the vinaigrette.

To make a vinaigrette:
Drain most of the vinegar out of the shallots, but leave just a little, add garlic paste, olive oil in a quantity you like and whisk well.

To assemble the salad:
Cut the tomatoes in half, put them in a bowl, add the Mozzarella bocconcini and black olives, vinaigrette and olive oil, salt and black pepper to taste. Mix well.
Serve with Pugliese type bread.

Note
1. Mozzarella bocconcini means small bites. They come in a tub with their own water and look like little balls. They are common to find in grocery stores.

Festa Of Mozzarella, Mushrooms, Tomatoes
Duration: 20 min.

Ingredients for 4 people
7 oz. of Mozzarella bocconcini[1]
8 oz. jar of store-bought roasted mushrooms (possibly without vinegar)
7 oz. of cherry tomatoes
1 shallot
extra virgin olive oil
a bunch of variety of spices: basil, marjoram, chives
salt and black pepper to your liking

Wash and chop all the ingredients. Cut the cherry tomatoes in half.

Assemble each plate separately.

In the centre of each plate arrange a few Mozzarella bocconcini.

Around Mozzarella place a few roasted mushrooms; go around the mushrooms and place cut tomatoes. If you roast your own mushrooms, the recipe will be healthier and it will taste better, but to save on preparation time, store-bought mushrooms are just fine.

In a jar add all the chopped spices with olive oil, salt and pepper to your liking, close with the lid and firmly shake the jar to obtain a creamy emulsion.

Pour it over the mozzarella, mushrooms and tomatoes. Adjust with the seasoning to your taste. Serve with a few toasted Pugliese bread slices.

Note
1. Mozzarella bocconcini are the small bite size mozzarella balls, sold in a tub with its own water. Available in many specialty stores and they are not expensive.

Cool Cucumber Salad
Duration: 15 min.

Ingredients for 4 people
4 cucumbers
1 small can of anchovies
a hand full of pitted black and green olives
extra-virgin olive oil to your liking
fresh squeezed lemon juice
salt and black pepper to taste

Peel the outer skin of the cucumbers, discard.

With the potato peeler make thin transparent slices lengthways. Peel all around the cucumber and stop when the seeds area shows up, discard it. Cucumber seeds are not easy to digest and they too watery for a salad.

Arrange all the thin shavings in a serving platter, let them rest for about ten minutes and they will produce some water.

Drain the water; add anchovies cut in small pieces, olives, salt and black pepper to your liking.

Drizzle extra-virgin olive oil and lemon juice. Be generous with the condiments, you want this simple salad to taste good!

Serve it on toast, or on Pugliese bread crostini, or alone as a delicious simple salad.

Roasted Onions With Olives
Duration: 50 min.

Ingredients for 4 people
1 onion per person
juice of ½ lemon
a hand full of pitted black olives
a hand full of capers
finely chopped mint leaves
arrucola leaves
extra-virgin olive oil
salt and black pepper to taste

Eliminate the outside skin of the onions.

Cut each onion in round slices of about ¼" keeping together all the rings.

Place them on a non-greased baking sheet. Make one swirl of olive oil on each slice. Season with salt and black pepper to taste.

Place them in the oven at 350° F for about forty minutes, or until golden brown, it very much depends on the oven type. Do not turn them over.

When done, place the roasted onion rings in a serving dish, season them with fresh squeezed lemon juice, salt and pepper to taste.

Add a hand full of black olives and capers, fresh mint leaves and a little more olive oil. Made it this way will be a nice salad and for many people it will be a new salad to taste.

If you want to serve crostini instead, prepare grilled or toasted crusty bread. When done place a few leaves of arrucola on top then the roasted onion salad, accompanied by a robust red wine and perhaps some veal cutlets.

Potato Stencils
Duration: 15 min.

Ingredients for 4 people
4 potatoes
4 egg whites
1 stick of butter
grated Parmigiano cheese
a hand full of chopped chives
salt and black pepper to taste

Boil the potatoes to make a conventional puree. Mash the potatoes through the ricer (ricer is a metal container with two handles and a perforated container in which to set one potato at the time; the plate on top presses the potato and it comes out through the holes at the bottom as strings and not mashed). The ricer is a common tool and easy to find in any commercial kitchen place.

To the potatoes strings add beaten egg whites, butter, a sprinkle of Parmigiano cheese (keep it delicate, don't overdue on cheese), salt and black pepper to your liking.

Save the egg yokes for something else.

Cut a raw potato in thin slices about 1/8" and reserve.

At this point, you need to make your own stencils with a hard type plastic sheet, like Mylar (a brand of strong, thin polyester film used in photography, recording tapes, and insulation, easy to find in craft and kitchen stores). Choose any design of your liking, a flower, a heart, or a water drop, keep it simple and don't get discouraged, this is an easy, fun design process.

Once the shape of the stencil has been decided and cut out of Mylar, place it on one of the raw potato slice and cut around the stencil you made. Transfer the potato stencil on a non-stick baking sheet. With a spreading knife wet in warm water, spread the potato mixture into the stencil in a thin layer, sprinkle chopped chives on this first layer. Cut the same shape of stencil the second time from another raw potato slice. Place it on top of the first layer. Again with the knife wet in warm water, spread thinly the potato mixture the second time on top of the second layer. Close with a third layer of a raw potato stencil in the same shape.

Bake at 400° F for about 10-15 minutes, making sure not to burn them.

Stencils will be golden in colour and crunchy. They can be served alone as a nice addition to the rest of the food on table, or on top of salad, as the last eatable decorative piece. They are truly marvellous!

Melon Handkerchief
Duration: 20 min.

Ingredients for 4 people

6 oz. Speck or Prosciutto
1 bunch of chives

1 honeydew melon
salt and pepper to your taste

Peel the melon, discard the seeds, cut slices and then bite size cubes.

Season the melon cubes with salt and black pepper as you like.

Crisscross a couple of Speck slices, lay a couple of melon cubes on top of the Speck in the centre.

Make packages by crossing one slice of the Speck over the cubed melon pieces, then bring the other Speck slice over and on top until all the four ends are closed and the package is formed.

Tight each packet of handkerchiefs with a few string of chives, just like making a ribbon on a package.

Align all the small handkerchiefs packets on a decorative plate; distribute the remaining melon cubes all around to add colour and flavour.

This is a fresh delicacy for any antipasto table!

—∞—

Skewers Extravaganza
Duration: 15 min.

Ingredients for 4 people

3 slices of Speck cut thick
yellow and red grapes
long wooden or steal skewers

2 slices of Scamorza or any smoked cheese
pearl onions in vinegar (store bought)
large oranges as needed

Cut in cubes Speck and Scamorza or any smoked cheese you like.

Wash the grape, drain the onions from the vinegar and pat them dry.

Skew each ingredient one by one in the order you like, until all the ingredients are used up. I would line up the ingredients by colours: speck, grape, cheese.

To assemble the skewers, cut both ends of an oranges to make them stable, cut the oranges in half, stick all the skewers inside of each half oranges and place them in the middle of the appetizers table for a stunning presentation.

Skewers Extravaganza

Farm Style Artichokes
Duration: 50 min.

Ingredients for 4 people
4 artichokes
1 onion finely sliced
5 peeled tomatoes
3 tablespoons of capers
5 or 6 tablespoons of olive oil
2 or 3 fillets of anchovy
a hand full of breadcrumbs
salt, black pepper to taste

Prepare a bowl with acidulate water, meaning with squeezed lemon juice and lemon peels. This water serves the purpose of preventing discoloration of the artichokes. At the end of handling the artichokes, the lemon peels can be used to rub on the hands that in the meantime have probably been stained from handling the artichokes.

Cut the pointed end of each artichoke.

Pool the hard, dark green leaves until reaching the pale, tendered part of the artichokes.

Cut the stems and peel the outside fibrous skin until reaching the tender green part. Cut them in thin rectangular strips.

Split the artichokes in half and cut off the feathery center called the "choke".

As you cut along, put all artichoke pieces in the bowl of water and lemons for about fifteen minutes.

In a pot bring salted water to a boil, add the artichokes.

Cook at medium fire for about 20 minutes, or until fork tender, but not soft.

Keep a good consistency.

In a frying pan sauté one onion in olive oil for about 3 to 4 minutes. Before the onion gets too translucent add the cooked artichokes.

Season with salt and black pepper to taste.

Cover the frying pan and cook them for about 8-10 minutes at medium fire.

Add peeled tomatoes; continue the cooking for about 10 more minutes until the sauce has thickened.

Finish the cooking with the capers, the anchovies cut in small pieces and breadcrumbs for five more minutes. Breadcrumbs will add texture.

Prepare "**pane unto**" (oiled bread) which is crusty bread toasted in the oven first, spread garlic clove, drizzle olive oil, season with salt and pepper.

Serve with a glass of rose' or red wine. It can also be made into a pasta dish.

Marbleized Vegetable Terrine
Duration: 60 min.
overnight in the refrigerator

Ingredients for 4 people

2 fresh mozzarella balls	balsamic vinegar	2 eggplants
a few basil leaves	2 red bell peppers	2 zucchini
extra-virgin olive oil	salt and black pepper to taste	2 tomatoes

Wash, slice and brush all the vegetables with olive oil, except bell peppers. Place them on a baking sheet. Bake at 350° F. or until golden brown.

Place the peppers whole on a baking sheet and roast in the oven at 350° F for about 25-30 minutes, or until scorched on all of the sides. Check often, making sure not to burn them. To cool them when done and to retain the moisture, place a plastic bag over them. As soon as they are manageable to the touch, remove the plastic bag, peel the skin off the peppers, take the seeds out and set them aside.

With your fingers (do not need a knife for the next operation) tear the pulp of the peppers into large strips of about 1" each.

Oil a terrine, line it with plastic wrap, let it hang over the rim, it will be helpful when you need to take the vegetables out of the terrine.

Form various layers with all the vegetables one by one, following a certain colour scheme. You want it to look pretty when you serve it.

Start with the eggplant layer, add a few slices of mozzarella, basil leaves, a few drops of balsamic vinegar, salt and pepper to taste. Continue with the roasted bell pepper slices; again add mozzarella, basil leaves, balsamic vinegar and salt and pepper. Continue the same way with the zucchini, the tomatoes and until all the vegetables are exhausted.

Make a swirl of olive oil at the end on top of all the vegetables.

Pick up the plastic wrap that is hanging over the rim of the terrine and cover the top of the vegetable layers.

Put a weight on top, such as a brick, or a couple of cans full of vegetables, or a bag of five pounds of beans. Refrigerate over night.

To take the vegetable composition out of the terrine

First open the plastic wrap on top, put a large plate face down on top of the terrine, turn the terrine up side down, pull the plastic wrap and discard it.

Drizzle olive oil, if you like and decorate it with a few Julienne mint leaves.

Serve it with boiled, or grilled shrimps and a fresh Pugliese bread.

It is summer on the Adriatic Sea!

Stuffed Eggplants
Duration: 60 min.

Ingredients for 4 people

2 Italian round eggplants	a hand full of toasted piñoli nuts
12 oz. of peeled tomatoes	2 eggs beaten
½ cup of olive oil	3 Mozzarella balls
8 oz. of cooked rice	a hand full of chopped parsley and chives
2 cloves of garlic	breadcrumbs
grated Romano or Pecorino cheese	salt and black pepper to taste
6 slices of Mortadella with pistachio nuts	

Cook the rice in the most convenient way to you. Reserve. Preheat oven at 375° F.

Wash the eggplants. Cut off only the top with the stem. Split them in half. With a sharp knife take out the interior spongy part and set it aside with salt while preparing all the ingredients. Salt will allow the bitter water of that sponge to come out.

In a baking dish put 4 or 5 chopped peeled tomatoes, ½ cup of water, 4 or 5 tablespoons of olive oil and chopped parsley. On top of these ingredients arrange the empty four halves of the eggplants. Bake uncovered for about 25 minutes.

Take the reserved spongy part, cut it first lengthwise and then chop it in small cubes. Chop all the ingredients and reserve. Toast the piñoli (pine nuts) without oil, beat the eggs and set aside.

In a skillet with ½ cup of olive oil, brown the cubed spongy part of the eggplants.

Keep the oil very hot on a high heat and the eggplants will not absorb lot of oil.

While browning the eggplant sponge, add 2 cloves of chopped garlic.

Turn the fire at medium high when the cubed eggplant sponge looks golden in colour.

In the same skillet, add 4 or 5 chopped tomatoes, cooked rice, toasted piñoli nuts (pine nuts), grated Romano or Pecorino cheese, coarsely chopped Mortadella, beaten eggs, chopped Mozzarella, salt and black pepper to taste. (Mortadella is a tasty Italian Bologna with pistachio nuts). Do not overdo on cheese, or Mozzarella, this is not a cheese dish!

Mix well and continue to sauté until all the ingredients have come together. Turn the fire off. Meanwhile the eggplant shells are soft and cooked, leave them in the baking pan.

Spoon this mixture of all ingredients into the baked eggplants halves; fill them up until all the ingredients are used up.

Top them with a little more chopped tomatoes, chopped parsley, a swirl of olive oil on each half, grated Romano, or Pecorino cheese and breadcrumbs.

In the bottom of the pan add more peeled tomatoes, ½ cup of water, a little more olive oil, salt and black pepper.

Bake at 375° F. until all the ingredients are amalgamated, the tops are golden and crispy and your house is filled with the aroma.

Serve one half stuffed eggplant per person with a bit of the cooking juice.

Note

Ground beef, ground veal, or prosciutto can be substituted in place of Mortadella.

If using ground meat, brown it separately from all the ingredients, drain the fat and then add it to rest of the ingredients.

Naples, Italy - The story of Via Foria

As I am writing this section on appetizers, a memory comes to mind:

Naples and a street called Via Foria. I experienced life in Bella Napoli as a young adult and came to fall in love with the city, folklore, the colours and smells of the streets.

Via Foria is a common looking street in Naples, but the folklore is worth a Hollywood film. It is located in the town centre near the American Embassy, close to the Lungomare, the beautiful Neapolitan promenade looking over the bay of Naples, dominated by Vesuvius, the sleeping volcano.

A peculiar characteristic of this street is the way one particular restaurant conducts its business. The street is very busy, dominated by noisy traffic and colourful loud people. The pavement of the street in front of the restaurant is occupied by tram tracks.

Due to lack of space inside the restaurant, literally a hole in the wall, the restaurant's owner places all of the tables outside in the street, on the sidewalk and on and around the tram tracks. Inside of the restaurant the tight working space is taken up by the brick pizza oven and by the home style stove. The same tight space is shared by the busy waiters who dispatch orders to the tables outside and by customers waiting for their food ordered to go who can't wait to leave because it is really hot in there.

Aside from what goes on inside the restaurant, outside its doors one of the family member attends large caldrons with steaming octopi cooking in their own juice, in addition to black mussels cooked in garlic and oil sauce called "impepata di cozze".

In the wintertime especially, when it's really cold, people sit out there under the dim streetlights and sip the octopus broth. It is cozy to sit close to each others. People say it fights the cold to taste this savoury, peppery, spicy specialty made nowhere else in Italy. It warms up the hearts. A glass or two of wine, of course, hit the spot.

The characteristic of this restaurant, as I was saying, is that the tram makes stops in that street, right in front of the restaurant. Every time the tram approaches, the tables are moved away from the tram tracks, along with the people seated at those tables, until the tram lets the passengers on and off. After the tram departs, the tables go back again in the spot where they had been situated before and so are the people eating at those tables, until the next tram comes around again. Fortunately the city traffic is so congested that an hour can pass between round trips so most customers can sit quietly undisturbed. On the other hand, considering how Italians like to linger at restaurant tables, it will appear to them as if the tram comes around every ten minutes. Naturally the people get annoyed, throw their hands up in the air to complains and fuss, but no one leaves, they like the drama and the folklore at the same time. The food is good too.

This particular street restaurant seems to be more packed today than it was yesterday, always full of customers waiting to enjoy the delightful specialties offered by "mama" the cook and all her other home cooked dishes. While you are waiting to be served, try the "arancini" they are always ready and hot, or drink a few glasses of wine and forget the tram and the rest of the world. Some things in life cannot be changed.

Tuna and Tomatoes Salad
Duration: 15 min.

Ingredients for 4 people

2 cans of tuna in olive oil	2 teaspoons of capers	a few cherry tomatoes
a hand full olives (any kind)	2 stalks of celery	a hand full of basil leaves
2 spring onions	extra-virgin olive oil	2 cloves of garlic
juice of 1 lemon	1 yellow bell pepper	salt and pepper to taste
Italian Pugliese bread, or ciabatta bread		

Wash and chop all the ingredients very fine and all the same sizes.

Remove the tuna and oil from the cans and place it in a bowl with all the chopped ingredients.

Add olive oil, season with salt and black pepper to your liking.

Squeeze the juice of one lemon to complete the taste.

Eat it either on crostini, or as a salad.

—◆—

Tuna Pate'
Duration: 20 min.

Ingredients for 4 people

4 green onions	1 teaspoon of white wine vinegar
2 celery stalks	green olives pitted (any olives OK)
1 can of tuna in water	a hand full of capers
2 tomatoes	olive oil
2 tablespoons of cream cheese	Italian parsley
1 teaspoon of lemon juice	crusty Italian bread

Wash and chop all the ingredients. In a skillet with olive oil sauté green onions and celery at low heat until soften. Let it cool.

Drain the water from the tuna in the can and deseed the tomatoes.

In a food processor put all the ingredients. Process it until the mixture is smooth.

Place the mixture in a nice bowl; garnish it with chopped Italian parsley, capers and chopped olives.

Serve on crusty Italian bread or baguette or as a dip with celery sticks.

Salmon Carpaccio

Salmon Carpaccio
Duration: 15 min.

Ingredients for 4 people
store-bought smoked salmon and pre-sliced[1]
2 shallots and 4 or 5 green onions
1 cucumber
3 or 4 teaspoons of capers
a hand full of chopped olives
½ lemon juice freshly squeezed
extra-virgin olive oil
salt and black pepper to your taste

Chop shallots and green onions. Reserve.

With a potato peeler, peel completely off the outer skin of a cucumber. Keep on peeling the flesh of the cucumber the long way to make long and thin strips. Continue on all sides until the seeds are showing. Discard the seeds core, it is too watery and it will not be good for this recipes.

On the serving dish, place many slices of smoked salmon slightly overlapping each other. On top of the salmon slices add the onion chopped and fluffed up, cucumber strips all curled up, as they were ribbons, distribute capers and olives.

Drizzle extra-virgin olive oil and squeeze the juice of a ½ lemon over.

Season with salt and pepper to your liking.

Serve it with "grissini" Italian bread sticks, or a fresh baguette.

Note
1. It is possible to smoke your own salmon at home if the smoker is available in your kitchen. The only few items needed are a hand full of dill leaves and wet hickory wood chips, or wet branches of any fruit trees from your garden chopped in small pieces. It's so easy to smoke anything at home.

This recipe can also be done with fresh cod slightly steamed or raw, the lemon juice will cook it.

Baked And Stuffed Mussels Pie
Duration: 40 min.

Ingredients for 4 people
1.5 lb. of mussels (frozen OK)
1 bag of shrimps (frozen OK)
6 eggs
1 cup of milk
4 to 5 tablespoons of breadcrumbs
a hand full of Italian parsley
olive oil to grease the baking dish
salt and black pepper to taste

Clean the mussel shells from ocean impurities, pull out any stringy fibres and rinse them in salty water. Peel and de-vein shrimps.

Beat the eggs, season with salt and pepper, add breadcrumbs and mix well.

Oil a shallow baking pie pan and place the egg mixture inside.

Arrange all the mussels and shrimps in the egg mixture.

Bake at about 350-375° F for about 20-25 minutes, or until the egg mixture is coagulated and the top is brown.

Present the baked mussels pie decorated with the empty shells of the mussels all around the edge of the pie.

Rustic Mussels Cocotte
Duration: 35 min.

Ingredients for 4 people
2 large leeks
3 cloves of chopped garlic
1 small pack of cherry tomatoes split in half
4 oz. of peeled tomatoes
1/3 cup of dry white wine
1.5 lb. of any clams
1.5 lb. of mussels
6 oz. of Capocollo[1] or any ham, cut into equal size strips
a hand full of chopped fresh Italian parsley
a hand full of fresh basil leaves
3 tablespoons extra-virgin olive oil
salt and chili pepper to your liking

Cut the leeks lengthwise and wash the impurities that are often found hiding in the centre. Thinly slice crosswise. Chop garlic and split the cherry tomatoes in half. Reserve.

Scrub clams and mussels, take the bird out of the mussels (stringy part found on one side of the mussels) and wash all the shellfish in salty water.

Heat oil in heavy large pot over medium heat. Add leeks and garlic and sauté until translucent, about 10 minutes. Add first wine and allow it to evaporate, then add all the tomatoes.

Cook for about ten minutes while the alcohol evaporates.

Add clams. Cover and cook five minutes. Add mussels, cover and cook until clams and mussels are all open, about 5 minutes longer (discard any shellfish that do not open).

Mix in Capocollo strips, parsley and basil leaves.

Season with salt and chili pepper to your taste.

Cook for ten more minutes covered.

Shrimps can be substitute in place of clams and mussels.

Note
1. Capocollo is an Italian sausage type made from pork shoulder, seasoned and cured. It is made to eat in sandwiches; occasionally we use it in cooking, just like any cured meat or sausages. Find it at Italian markets.

Stuffed Mussels

Duration: 45 min.

Ingredients for 4 people

2 lb. of shelled mussels[1]	a hand full of Italian parsley
breadcrumbs	Parmigiano cheese
1 or 2 diced tomatoes deseeded	salt and black pepper to your liking
2 or 3 cloves of minced garlic	extra-virgin olive oil
2 eggs beaten	1 pack of rock salt

Clean the mussel shells from ocean impurities, pull out any stringy fibres and rinse them in salty water.

Put them in a large pot with ¾ cup of water, cover with a lid. Turn the fire on medium and let the shells open. Cool down, leave the mussels on the half shell, discard the other half.

To prepare the filling:

In a bowl mix breadcrumbs, minced garlic, parsley, small pieces of diced tomatoes without the seeds, salt and black pepper to taste, grated Parmigiano cheese. Beat eggs and mix in with the ingredients.

Season the mixture to your liking.

Fill the bottom of an ovenproof clay pot, or any baking sheet with rock salt. The rock salt will prevent the shells from wobbling.

Align each mussel on top of the rock salt. Spoon the mixture to fill the mussels, drizzle a swirl of olive oil and a light sprinkle of Parmigiano cheese.

Bake them in a preheated oven at 350° F for about fifteen minutes until the eggs are coagulated.

Note

1. To test if the fresh mussels are really fresh and good, bang two together. The mussel that opens and closes is a good one; the mussel that remains either open or closed is not a good one and should be discarded. For this recipe I **always** use fresh, live mussels. Frozen green mussels are OK, but the taste of the sea will not be there.

Stuffed Mussels

Seafood Canapé
Duration: 15 min.

Ingredients for 4 people
American bread sliced
2 eggs
1 can or packaged salmon
one bunch of Italian parsley
a few lettuce leaves
½ lemon juice
a few teaspoons of capers
chives needles
extra-virgin olive oil
salt and pepper to your liking

Hard boil the eggs and peel the shells off when cooled.
Toast the bread slices.
Take the salmon out of the can or package and crumble it with a fork.
Season it with lemon juice, olive oil, salt and pepper. Add capers.
On each bread slice arrange one lettuce leaf, a spoon of the seasoned salmon pulp, a few slices of hard-boiled eggs; sprinkle parsley and chives needles all over and serve them.

Wine:
Vermentino di Gallura a wine from Sardegna, or a chilled Pinot Bianco from the Northern Italian region of Veneto.

Exotic Small Bites
Duration: 25 min.

Ingredients for 4 people

1 lb. of mild Italian sausage	1 whole pineapple
a hand full of basil leaves	extra-virgin olive oil
salt and black pepper to taste	toothpicks

Cut the sausage in round small bites, sauté in a skillet with olive oil until brown. Set aside.

Cut the pineapple in small triangles, season with salt and pepper and sauté in a skillet with olive oil, or grill them under the oven broiler until golden brown.

Assemble sausage bites and pineapple triangles on toothpicks with one basil leave in between each piece. Align them in a serving plate.

Any simpler than this would be a crime!

—∿—

Grilled Brochettes
Duration: 15 min.

Ingredients for 4 people

1 lb. of fresh figs	1 lb. of cumquats (tangerines OK)
1 lb. of cherry tomatoes	½ walnut for each fig
1 lb. of Italian Prosciutto di Parma	extra-virgin olive oil
(domestic Prosciutto OK)	salt and pepper to your liking
mixed spices: sage, rosemary, thyme	metal skewers

Cut the figs in half, insert ½ walnut inside of each one. Wrap each fig inside of one slice of Prosciutto and roll it close as a package. Align on a skew one stuffed Prosciutto roll, one cumquat, one cherry tomato, until the skewer is full. Continue until all the ingredients are gone and all the skewers are filled. Brush each skewer with a mixture of olive oil and spices mentioned in the list. Grill for only 5 to 7 minutes.

The spices mixture, other than the one mentioned in the ingredients list, can be made of a variety of combinations. Here there is one more combination for you: mint, dill, lemon grass, ginger and garlic.

Stuffed Small Chicken Rolls
Duration: 40 min.

Ingredients for 4 people
1 chicken breast per person
2 lb. of spinach
grated Parmigiano cheese
Mozzarella cheese
2 garlic cloves
3 or 4 oz. of pine nuts
freshly grated nutmeg
5 or 6 tablespoons of olive oil
½ cup of white wine
salt and pepper to taste
cotton thread and toothpicks

Wash the spinach, chop the garlic, sauté them together in olive oil until soft. Squeeze the water out of the spinach produced during cooking.

Toast the pine nuts without oil very briefly and set aside.

Chop the Mozzarella cheese in small cubes and grate the Parmigiano.

Mix all the ingredients together in a bowl.

Butterfly each chicken breast, flatten a bit with the meat pounder. To butterfly a piece of meat means to simply insert the knife inside the thinner part of the meat and cut through the flesh evenly until the thicker part is reached. Do not cut all the way through to the other end, stop at about ¼" before the edge. Open the meat like a butterfly and pound to flatten the centre and all around the flesh.

Fill the centre of each breast with all the ingredients.

Season to your liking with salt, pepper and freshly grated nutmeg.

Roll it tight keeping everything inside. Secure the meat package by closing it with a cooking cotton thread and toothpicks.

Place the stuffed chicken breasts in a skillet with olive oil and brown them on all sides. Add ½ cup of white wine to flavour, or beer, let the alcohol evaporate, then finish the breasts in the oven for only 8-10 minutes in the same skillet if the handle is not plastic, or transfer them to a baking pan. Bake at 450° F.

Cut thread away from the meat, then cut the stuffed breasts in diagonal slices about ¾" thick and arrange them nicely in the plate with some vegetables and potatoes around. One stuffed breast per person can also be served if you have healthy eaters at your table.

Chicken Cacciatore (Hunter Style)
Duration: 35 min.

Ingredients for 4 people
1 whole chicken
3 garlic cloves
½ cup of olive oil
a few leaves of thyme, sage and rosemary
½ cup of white wine
4 or 5 peeled tomatoes
vegetable or chicken stock
salt and black pepper to taste

Cut the chicken in small pieces. Wash it well and eliminate all the fat tissue and skin. Include the interiors and the neck in the cooking process[1], they are delicious and add flavour.

Brown the chicken pieces on all the sides, add all the seasoning previously chopped and garlic cloves chopped.

Wet it with ½ cup of white wine. Let the alcohol evaporate.

Add peeled tomatoes and cover the chicken with stock, or water as needed.

This is not chicken in a red sauce; the peeled tomatoes are only intended to give colour to the dish. Simmer at low fire and covered until the chicken is totally cooked. It makes a very tasty appetizer.

To serve it as a dinner, add saffron rice, green leaves vegetable, like chard or spinach and sautéed carrots. There you have it, a very nice colour combination.

Note
1. Another way to use the interiors parts of the chicken is to sauté them in a hot iron skillet with a couple of spoons of olive oil, chopped garlic, thyme, sage and rosemary, seasoned with salt and pepper. Brown them on all sides and eat them warm. They are a delicious snack.

Bresaola And Cheese Rolls
Duration: 15 min.

Ingredients for 4 people
2 oz. of Mascarpone cheese
12 slices of Bresaola[1]
chopped black olives
mixed lettuce leaves
juice of 1 lemon
1 tablespoon of capers
3 or 4 tablespoons of extra-virgin olive oil
lemon slices to garnish
salt and black pepper to taste

Whip Mascarpone into a cream; add chopped olives, season with salt and pepper.

Season the mixed lettuce with olive oil and lemon juice, season to your liking.

Arrange it on a serving platter.

Lay all Bresaola slices flat on the working surface. Arrange, the short way, one teaspoon of Mascarpone cheese, 1 or 2 dry lettuce leaves, roll each slice.

Place all the Bresaola rolls on a bed of the mixed lettuce; add capers around and lemon slices to garnish the serving plate.

Each person will have 3 rolls; three is always the perfect number.

This appetizer can be a complement to a luscious platter of Italian cured meats, cheeses and olives. Include also all the products conserved in olive oil, such as: stuffed peppers, tuna, artichokes, mushrooms and sun-dried tomatoes.

There you have it a real Italian treat.

Note

1.   Breasaola is cured beef meat from Valtellina a northern area of Italy.

To be authentic, Breasola must have the certification IGP (Identificazione Geografica Protetta), which assures that the meat is produced in a protected geographical area.

The origin of the name Bresaola is not certain. It could be deriving form the northern dialect word brasa (brazier) due to the primitive method of drying Bresaola in rooms heated with braziers. This method is no longer in use.

Roasted Chicken in Pineapple Shells

Roasted Chicken in Pineapple Shells
Duration: 70 min.

Ingredients for 4 people
1 whole chicken
½ pineapple shell per person
1 extra pineapple for the marinade
extra-virgin olive oil
salt and black pepper

Cut the chicken in the size pieces of your liking. Take the skin off, wash and reserve for the marinade.

Marinade:
Carve the pulp out of the pineapple shell, cut in small pieces and place it in the food processor along with 2 jalapeño peppers, cilantro (parsley is OK to use, if you don't like cilantro flavour), 3 or 4 garlic cloves, juice of ½ lemon, 2 or 3 tablespoons of olive oil and salt to your taste. Mix well. Transfer it to a bowl.

Place the cut chicken pieces in this marinade for about 30 minutes.

Roast the marinated chicken in the oven at 400° F. until the chicken is golden brown, about 40-45 minutes, depending on the oven. Grilling the chicken pieces is also a good thing to do with this marinade.

During the time chicken is roasting, prepare the pineapple for the grill.

This phase will take much shorter cooking time, start it almost at the end of the chicken cooking time.

Split all the pineapples in half the long way. Carve out the pineapple flesh very close to the shell, but leave a bit of the pineapple pulp around.

Cut the pulp in medium size triangles, roll them in olive oil, salt and pepper and grill them either on a grill pan for the stove, or on an outdoor grill.

Make grill marks, they looks so good on any food. Reserve for later.

Mix together roasted chicken pieces and grilled pineapple triangles, place them in the empty pineapple shells, add a swirl of fresh olive oil, adjust the seasoning and serve.

All the half pineapples filled with the roasted chicken pieces when placed in a large serving platter can take center stage on the appetizers table, or they can be served one per person as a dinner. Either way, you will surprise your guests with this presentation and with the burst of flavours.

This dish is good to serve warm.

Veal Steaks In Cartouche
Duration: 40 min.

Ingredients for 4 people
1 veal steak per person (small size, no bones)
a mixture of spices: sage, thyme, garlic, chives
½ cup dry white wine
extra-virgin olive oil
salt and pepper to taste
aluminium foil

Flatten each steak to make them a bit thinner.

Chop all the spices and spread tightly packed over the veal steaks.

In a skillet briefly sauté the small steaks, wet them with the white wine, evaporate the alcohol.

Prepare aluminium foil in squares, place each veal steak on the foil with the cooking juices, close and place the small packages in the preheated oven at 375° F for about 15-20 minutes.

Place all the cartouches closed in a serving plate.

Let your guests open their own package and surprise them.

Note

Chicken can be substituted in place of veal.

Mortadella Frittata Rolls
Duration: 40 min.

Ingredients for 4-6 people
8 eggs
1/3 cup of milk
grated Pecorino cheese
a hand full of fresh tarragon, or Italian parsley
a hand full of fresh chives
½ lb. of Mortadella[1] thinly cut
½ lb. of Mozzarella in water
vegetable oil as needed to fry
salt and black pepper to taste
toothpicks

Chop the tarragon very fine, or parsley whichever is available, grate Pecorino cheese and slice the mozzarella very thin. Reserve.

In a bowl beat the eggs, add all the ingredients at once and season with salt and black pepper to your liking. Egg mixture must not be runny, if it is add more cheese.

In a skillet warm up 2 tablespoons of vegetable oil. Spoon in the egg mixture, one spoon at the time to make pancakes like disks of about 4" diameter and it will take 2 spoons of mixture. If you want them bigger, spoon more egg mixture in the oil.

Continue to fry until the egg mixture has been exhausted. Add vegetable oil as needed while frying.

Stack them up in a plate with absorbent paper and let them cool.

On each frittata cake, place one thin slice of Mortadella and one thin slice of Mozzarella cheese. Roll it on itself, close the edge with 2 or 3 toothpicks to secure the ingredients inside.

Before serving, preheat oven at 375° F.

Bake only until the mozzarella is half way melted, about 10 minutes, or less.

Serve the small frittata rolls as appetizers, or as a second course with a colourful salad.

Note
1. Mortadella is the Italian version of Bologna. It comes with pistachio nuts. The domestic made in USA does not have pistachios. If Mortadella is not of your taste, substitute it with any ham of your liking.

Frittata Austerity
Duration: 40 min.

Ingredients for 4 people

4 Yukon gold potatoes	1 onion
4 oz. of pancetta[1]	6 eggs
Pecorino, or Romano cheese to your liking	a hand full of Italian parsley
5 or 6 tablespoons of olive oil	salt and black pepper

Cut the potatoes in thin strips. Brown them in a few drops of olive oil. Set aside.

In another frying pan sauté sliced onion and pancetta cut in cubes.

Beat the eggs, season with salt and pepper and parsley.

Transfer all the ingredients in the skillet with the potatoes, add the beaten eggs. Cover and let the eggs coagulate.

At this point the frittata is cooked on the bottom and needs to cook on the other side. There are two ways to proceed.

Method #1:

If the skillet has oven proof handle, place it in the oven and bake the frittata uncovered at 375° F until golden brown on top. Discard the rest of the recipes.

Serve with shavings of the same type of cheese used in the frittata.

Method #2:

In order to cook the other side, the frittata needs to be turned over.

Put a plate face down on top of the open skillet and turn it over, be careful not to spill hot oil over your hands. Use oven mittens with this operation. The plate must be of a larger diameter than the skillet.

Return the frittata to the skillet. Brown the other side.

Serve with shavings of the same type of cheese used in the frittata.

Method #2 makes the crust on both sides. I like that.

Note

1. Pancetta is the Italian bacon cured in salt and coarse black pepper. It is sold in rolls tied with a cotton rope. It can be eaten raw in sandwiches sliced very thinly. If used in cooking it is better to cube it. If pancetta is not available in your area, substitute it with good quality bacon.

Leeks and Gorgonzola Frittata
Duration: 40 min.

Ingredients for 4 people
6 eggs
1 leak finely chopped
2 oz. of bacon, or Italian prosciutto
Gorgonzola cheese cut in small pieces
½ cup of milk
5 or 6 tablespoons of olive oil
a hand full of roasted almonds slivered
1 bunch of chives
salt and black pepper to taste

Split the leaks lengthways in the centre and wash well, they conceal a lot of soil. Finely slice them. Reserve. Chop the bacon or prosciutto and reserve.

In a bowl beat the eggs, add all the ingredients, except the leaks, whisk well.

Set aside.

In a skillet sauté the leaks in olive oil until translucent. Combine the leaks to the mixture of eggs and all the ingredients. Brown the frittata on one side covered.

At this point the frittata is cooked on the bottom and needs to cook on the other side. There are two ways to proceed.

Method #1:
If the skillet has oven proof handle, place it in the oven and bake the frittata uncovered at 375° F until golden brown on top. Discard the rest of the recipes.

Serve with slivered roasted almonds and chives needles on top.

Method #2:
In order to cook the other side, the frittata needs to be turned over.

Put a plate face down on top of the open skillet and turn it over, be careful not to spill hot oil over your hands. Use oven mittens with this operation. The plate must be of a larger diameter than the skillet.

Return the frittata to the skillet. Brown the other side.

Serve with slivered roasted almonds and chives needles on top.

Method #2 makes the crust on both sides. I like that.

Pasta Frittata

Duration: 40 min.

,s for 4 people

6 eggs

Parmigiano cheese grated

1 bunch of chives, or Italian parsley

2 oz. per person of any pasta

5 or 6 tablespoons of olive oil

salt and chili pepper to taste

The most important result to achieve in this recipe is a golden brown crunchy crust on both sides of the frittata. This is an unpretentious recipe that gives you an opportunity to reuse leftover cooked pasta, or to use all the half opened pasta packages in your pantry that are not enough to do anything else.

If leftover cooked pasta is available, whether it is pasta with meat sauce, pasta with vegetables, or fish, the original condiment will give the flavour of the frittata. It will be mixed in with the egg mixture, grated Parmigiano cheese, seasoned with salt and hot pepper to your liking, chopped parsley and nothing else. Brown it in the skillet with olive oil.

Otherwise, if leftover cooked pasta is not available, cook the pasta as usual **al dente**. Drain the water well.

In a bowl beat the eggs; add cooked pasta. Season generously with salt and hot chili pepper, indulge with grated Parmigiano cheese and chopped parsley.

You want it to be savoury, because it is poor of ingredients. Transfer everything to a skillet with olive oil and brown the bottom first. Don't stir, don't shake the skillet, it needs to make a crust.

At this point the frittata is cooked on the bottom and needs to cook on the other side. There are two ways to proceed.

Method #1:

If the skillet has oven proof handle, place it in the oven and bake the frittata uncovered at 375° F until golden brown on top. Discard the rest of the recipes.

Serve with slivered roasted almonds and chives needles on top.

Method #2:

In order to cook the other side, the frittata needs to be turned over.

Put a plate face down on top of the open skillet and turn it over, be careful not to spill hot oil over your hands. Use oven mittens with this operation. The plate must be of a larger diameter than the skillet.

Return the frittata to the skillet. Brown the other side.

Serve with slivered roasted almonds and chives needles on top.

Method #2 makes the crust on both sides. I like that.

Baked Ricotta Cheese
Duration: 50 min.

Ingredients for 4 people

6 oz. of ricotta per person
a hand full of black olives chopped
extra-virgin olive oil as needed

a few slices of prosciutto diced
salt and coarse ground black pepper to taste
1 bunch of chives

Preheat oven at 400° F.

Discard the water from the ricotta in the tub. In a bowl thoroughly mix the ricotta with all the ingredients. Transfer the mixture into a buttered clay-baking dish, or into single ramekins, this way each portion of ricotta will have the same size and appearance. Drizzle olive oil on top, as liked.

Bake in the oven for about 30-40 minutes until the top is crispy and golden brown.

Be careful not to overcook the ricotta, or it will break and become grainy. If this happens, remove the ricotta from the oven and cool it slightly. To finish the cooking, place it under the broiler and let the top brown. Decorate it with chives needles.

Accompany it with a salad of mixed tomatoes.

—⟋⟍—

Fried Olive In Tomato Salsa
Duration: 20 min.

Ingredients for 4 people

½ lb. of black olives in water not treated
8 oz. can of peeled tomatoes
2 tablespoons of olive oil
salt, black pepper to taste

a hand full of Italian parsley
one day old country bread
2 cloves of garlic
Parmigiano shavings

Drain the water out of the olives. Chop the garlic and the peeled tomatoes.

In a skillet sauté garlic and black olives in olive oil and at medium fire, until the olives start to become crinkled. Add chopped peeled tomatoes. Cook for about ten minutes.

Season with salt and black pepper to taste. Be generous with the condiments.

Lay a few slices of stale country bread at the bottom of the serving platter.

Fill up the platter with the fried olives in the tomato salsa.

Sprinkle parsley finely chopped and complete the dish by decorating with Parmigiano shavings.

Roasted Vegetable Frittata
Duration: 50 min.

Ingredients for 4 people
1 zucchini
1 red or yellow bell pepper
1 small red onion
4 large white mushrooms
6 eggs
2 or 3 tablespoons of olive oil
1 package of artichoke hearts (frozen OK)
non-stick cooking spray
5 oz. of any soft cheese (with garlic and herbs OK)
2 teaspoons of milk
grated Parmigiano cheese
salt and black pepper to your taste

Preheat oven to 450° F. Slice zucchini in ¼" inch thick; cut the bell pepper in small strips, chop onion and mushrooms. Cook artichoke hearts according to the directions on the package; drain the water if any and mix in with the rest of the vegetables.

In a large, shallow baking pan, combine all the vegetables. Drizzle olive oil; sprinkle salt and black pepper. Toss well to coat. Bake, uncovered, in the preheated oven for about 25 minutes or until tender, stirring once halfway through baking time.

Meanwhile with an electric mixer beat semi-soft cheese on medium speed until smooth, add milk and beaten eggs. Season to your liking. Take out the roasted vegetables. Reduce oven temperature to 400° degrees F.

Lightly coat another baking pan with non-stick cooking spray.

Drop in beaten eggs, cheese and roasted vegetables with its own cooking juices. Add grated Parmigiano cheese. Mix well and adjust seasoning.

Bake again 400° F. for about 20 minutes or until the top is golden and the egg mixture is coagulated.

Bari, Italy – Via Amendola – Brick public oven

To write this piece, I had to open a long road in the valley of my memory to let out the images, the aromas and the events tied to the tasty food my mother and grandmother prepared long ago. I was about seven or eight years old, I lived in Via Amendola, in Bari. After we moved to a newly built residence in a better neighbourhood, in the Carrassi area, the home of my childhood was replaced by a modern glass building with offices on every flight.

At that time, not every family had an oven in their home, but baking food was still a must. In each borough there were legitimate businesses "the public ovens" that made their living with baking people's food. The public ovens were made of bricks built inside of a large store space. There was nothing else in these stores, only ovens, lot of heat and a cranky, easily irritable owner.

The "garzone" a store helper was put to do a variety of tasks, sweeping the floor, pickup and deliver the food from and to people's homes.

He arrived at each home with a long and flat piece of wood board of about 12"-15" wide under his arm and a thick towel in his hands. He would twist the towel in a round shape and place it on his head onto which the guy would set the wood board and all the baking pans aligned one after the other. His ability was to balance the pans on his head and not to drop the goods on the floor. Sometimes the garzone came on a cheap, old, run down bicycle without breaks. He loaded all the balking goods on his head, how he never fell, or lost his load is still a mystery to me and used his well worn out, seasoned feet as the breaks.

Each specialty carried a name of the client, the name of the food to be baked and the time needed to bake a particular food. The lady of the house gave him the information.

The owner of the brick oven was also an expert on the cooking time, he knew exactly how long each food needed to cook and he charged accordingly. The "cottura" (baking time) was his fee, based on the cooking time and the value of the food. A dish with lot of ingredients was more expensive to bake than a specialty with fewer ingredients.

The ritual question the client asked was: "Quanto devo portare e a che ora devo venire?" How much do I bring and when do I come back to get it, if the client wanted to pick up the food. The baked food was picked up sharp at the time the baker said, not one minute later and that is because the food had to go hot directly from the public oven onto the table to feed the family.

A large napkin, or a small tablecloth was wrapped around the cooked goods and a knot was tied on the centre top of the pan to create a handle. This was the way to carry the food out of the public oven. It was a way to keep it safe, out of the street dust and the only way not to get burn on the way home.

In order to avoid contamination of flavours and aromas, all the savoury food, and all fish and meat dishes were baked in the morning, all the sweets were baked after 3:00 o'clock in the afternoon. That was the rule of the public oven baker.

The afternoon baking was more of a social gathering between the people of the borough. Nobody was in a rush to take home the sweets. They were prepared in advance for the holidays.

Every sweet dish, cookies, cakes and pies had a distinct mark of the family on top of the goods to avoid mistaking the same dish with a different family.

The savoury dishes brought to the oven were called "tiedde" and were divided in primi piatti (first course specialties), secondi piatti (second course specialties) and all the Christmas or Easter sweets.

The most common of the tiedde in Puglia was the Timballo, alias pasta al forno. It was made of mezzi ziti pasta, with tomato sauce, mozzarella, small cute meatballs previously fried, mortadella with pistachio nuts cut in very thin slices, the whole dish covered with breadcrumbs and cherry tomatoes cracked in half.

Continue

The second best savoury tiedda was Patate, Riso e Cozze (Potatoes, Rice and Mussels), a typical dish of Puglia. Stuffed Eggplants, Stuffed Bell Peppers, or Potato Gateau were in line of importance.

Every family made the savoury pizza type called Calzone, with either meat or vegetables. Calzone was stuffed with meat and mozzarella, or with leaks, olives and anchovies. These were the very typical types of Calzone, but many more specialties were created.

The tiedde with meats of lamb, rabbit or pork were considered a delicacy and brought to the public oven for Sunday dinners and holidays. During the week, people of Puglia ate more frugally and very simple food with less calories. Simple food was all people could afford, counting calories was not a known way of living.

The snack type food saw the way to the public oven too. Taralli, or Italian pretzels, were the most common of all, filled with black pepper corn, or fennel seeds, a small delight of which is impossible to eat only one. The recipe of Taralli is in this book.

The baking of the breads only happened once a week, as the homemade bread could be kept a long time in the credenza. Each loaf was about three pounds and each person ate around 350 gr. of bread a day (a little over 12 oz). Each loaf also carried the family mark.

Then there was the parade of the Christmas and Easter sweets:

Castagnelle, Pasta Reale, Biscotti of all types and shapes. We ate them in the morning with caffe' e latte, or with a simple espresso. Easter Scarcelle with a boiled egg in the centre was also eaten in the morning for breakfast long after Easter celebration was over.

Most of these recipes are in this book.

Parmigiano Bread Sticks
Duration: 40 min.

Ingredients for 6-8 people

1 loaf baguette-style French bread	non-stick cooking spray
½ cup olive oil	¾ cup grated Parmigiano cheese

Use more baguettes for a higher number of people.

Preheat oven to 375° F. Cut the long baguette in half. Cut each half lengthwise in half, then into ¼" - to ½" strips. Make sure to cut each strip in such a way to have a crust on each strip.

Line a long baking pan with foil and lightly coat with cooking spray. Try the bread stick baking sheet, made with useful slots for each strip and holes for a good crispiness.

It is very appropriate.

Arrange half of the breadsticks in a single layer. Drizzle olive oil over.

Using a pair of tongs, carefully turn breadsticks to coat with oil.

Sprinkle Parmigiano cheese.

Bake for 10 -12 minutes or until browned and crispy. Repeat with remaining breadsticks, oil, and cheese. Transfer to a large serving bowl or platter.

Bread sticks can be served alone or as an accompaniment to any sauce or dipping of your liking, or even with prosciutto wrapped around them.

I doubt there will be any leftover, but in case there is place the leftover breadsticks in a covered container and store at room temperature for 2 days or in the freezer up to one month.

—ɷ—

To make roasted pepper dipping sauce for the bread sticks

4 red bell peppers	2 shallots
extra-virgin olive oil	½ cup of dry white wine
4 cloves of garlic	a hand full of Italian parsley
2 teaspoons of capers	salt and ground black pepper to your liking

Scorch 4 red bell peppers in the oven or on the grill. Peel the burnt skin, discard seeds and drain any possible water formed inside the peppers.

Place them in the food processor with all the ingredients at once except capers.

Process it into a creamy sauce. Add capers and mix.

Makes about 1-1/2 cup.

Taralli

Taralli
(Italian Pretzels)
Duration: 5-6 hours for rising
30 min. for boiling and baking

Ingredients for 6-8 people
32 oz. of semola flour
7.5 fluid oz. of olive oil
1 pack of beer yeast
a pinch of salt
3 oz. of fennel seeds
white dry wine as needed

Spread semola flour on the working surface. Make a well in the centre and slowly pour white wine to mix all the ingredients, yeast included.

Wine <u>must not be</u> chilled. Start with ½ cup of wine for mixing and continue adding wine little by little at a time to finish the kneading and make a ball of medium hard consistency.

Cut small pieces of about 6" of diameter each and keep them under a plastic wrap to avoid hardening. Each 6" piece will be cut again in 2 smaller pieces.

Roll each one into long snakes and then cut final pieces of about 3" each.

Make a ring out of each 3" pieces and close by pressing firmly both ends of the dough together.

Clear a large surface like a kitchen counter or a table and as taralli are shaping up, place them on a wax paper, or silicon mats and leave them to rest covered for 5 or 6 hours.

In a pot bring salted water to a boil. Drop in the taralli, for only a few minutes, when they come up to the top means they are done and can be scooped up with a perforated ladle. Drain them on a cotton kitchen cloth without fuzz, otherwise the fuzz will stick to the wet taralli.

Place them on a non-stick baking sheet and bake them at 355° F. for about 15-18 minutes, or until golden brown, depending on the oven. Check often to avoid burning them. Oven door can be opened to check.

Rest them to cool on a wooden board, or on the kitchen granite counter.

Note
Taralli can also be made as sweet pretzels, but one egg must be added in the mixture and at the end sprinkle powdered sugar over.

Stuffed Pizza

Stuffed Pizzas

Duration: 3 hrs. for rising dough
50 min. to stuff and bake

Ingredients for 6-8 people

14 oz. of wheat flour
½ cube of beer yeast
1 or 2 teaspoons of sugar
1 egg white

¼ cup of olive oil
warm water as needed to mix
1 teaspoon of salt

Method #1: To mix all the ingredients and turn it into a ball, it is OK to use a food processor. Put in the machine all the ingredients and mix until a ball is obtained. Pour water from the top of the processor in a small quantity at the time as needed. Let the machine form a ball.

Rest the dough to allow rising for about 2 hours in a warm place, away from wind draft and covered with a plastic wrap. It will double its size, bubbles will form on top. That means the dough is getting pliable and soft. After this time, rework and knead it again, let it rise for another hour. After three hours of rising, it will be ready to receive all the ingredients.

Method #2: Personally, I like to use my hands and my muscle strength.

On a working surface spread flour, make a well in the centre, add salt, oil, crumble beer yeast and spread it all over the flour along with the sugar. Starts kneading by adding a small amount of water first, about ½ cup in the middle of the well, then add more water as needed to turn all the ingredients into a kneaded ball.

Transfer the ball into an oiled bowl. Let the dough rise for about 2 hours in a warm place, away from wind draft and covered with a plastic wrap. It will double its size, bubbles will form on top. After this time, rework and knead it again, let it rise for another hour. After three hours of rising, it will be ready to receive all the ingredients.

Transfer on a working surface the ball of dough completely risen. Divide it in two pieces. Keep one piece of dough under plastic wrap to avoid hardening while working on the other piece.

With a rolling pin, roll out and stretch one piece of dough to fit the size of baking pan you are going to use. Oil the baking pan, lay over the stretched piece of dough and fill it with all ingredients of your liking. See below my suggested ingredient combinations.

Roll out and stretch the other piece of dough. Once it is stretched out to the same size of the baking pan, it will go on the top to cover the ingredients.

Pinch together the edge of the two dough pieces all around, with a fork poke holes all over the top to provide steam escape while baking.

Brush the top with either olive oil or an egg wash. To make egg wash, beat one egg white, add 1 tablespoon of water, mix well and brush it over any pie when you want to achieve a golden tone. Bake at 325° F for about 40 minutes, or depending on the oven, until the top is golden brown and the toothpick test comes out clean.

Stuffed Pizzas
Continue

Suggested ingredients for any stuffed pizzas

Suggestions #1: Ground beef previously cooked and drained of any possible fat; mozzarella cut in small bite sizes, 2 or 3 hard boiled eggs chopped coarsely, steamed spinach drained of its juices, salt and pepper to your taste.

Suggestions #2: Chopped asparagus sautéed in olive oil with garlic; chopped mozzarella and Prosciutto, a few peeled tomatoes, salt and pepper to your liking.

Suggestions #3: Sautéed spinach drained of its juices; four types of cheeses of your liking, salt and pepper to your taste.

Suggestions #4: Spread pesto sauce; top it with chopped mozzarella, black olives and peeled tomatoes, salt and pepper to your taste.

Suggestions #5: Mixed seafood sautéed in olive oil with garlic; chopped peeled tomatoes, black olives, capers, salt and pepper to your taste.

4 Seasons Pizza

4 Seasons Pizza

Duration: 2 hrs. 15 min. for rising
25 min. for baking

To make the "mother starter" from yeast for the pizza bread

In a bowl mix 1 cube of beer yeast, or 2 packs of dry yeast, 1 tablespoon of honey (granulated sugar OK), 3 or 4 tablespoons of all purpose white flour, warm water at a temperature between 105° and 110° F. The water must be poured in the mixture a little at the time while stirring with the fork, or a whisk. The mixture must be fluid, dense, but not hard. Do not add salt in this stage, otherwise it will react against the yeast. Cover the bowl with plastic wrap and let it rest in a warm non-ventilated place. The yeast will ferment and the mixture will double its size. It will be full of bubbles on top and will be very airy.

When this process happens, you have produced the so-called "mother" or "starter".

To make pizza bread

Ingredients to make the dough for 6-8 people
16 oz. of all-purpose flour
1-1/2 cup of semola flour
1/3 cup extra-virgin olive oil
2 tablespoons of salt or to your taste

On a counter surface, spread flour; mix in 2 tablespoons of salt. Make a well in the centre and place the mother starter just produced inside of the well with 1/3 cup of olive oil.

Near your working station set a container with warm water at a temperature between 105° and 110° F., which will be used during kneading. At this point work from the inside of the well toward the outside in a circular motion. Using a fork mix all the ingredients in the centre of the well, add water in small quantities and pick up some of the flour from around the centre. Work your way until the mother starter and the flour are well mixed, then use your hands. Make a firm ball by kneading for a few minutes.

Place the dough ball in a large, oiled bowl, cover it with plastic wrap and a cloth on top and set it in a warm non-ventilated place. Let it rise for about 1 hour.

I place the bowl under some covers and close the door of the room, so the dough can rest quietly. If the dough is nervous it will not rise.

After one hour of resting, rework the dough again, push down all the air, place the ball back into the oiled bowl and let it rest covered for another hour, under the covers in a warm place.

To save time, it is OK to use pre-made pizza dough. I have never done it. The point is to make food from scratch that will taste 100 percent better than the store-bought food and project yourself into a slow mood and slow food.

4 Seasons Pizza Continue

Ingredients to fill a 4 Seasons Pizza

peeled tomatoes	mozzarella
one bunch of fresh Italian parsley	prosciutto
mushrooms	artichokes in a jar with olive oil
garlic	salt and pepper to taste
black olives	extra-virgin olive oil
tuna in can with olive oil	one bunch of fresh basil leaves

The quantity of the ingredients for the top filling is up to you. Italian never overstuff their pizzas. Take that as a rule for a good pizza.

Wash the mushrooms, slice them coarsely, sauté in olive oil with garlic on high fire.

Add chopped parsley and salt at the very end.

Chop mozzarella, prosciutto and olives, deseed peeled tomatoes and get rid of the water, take out the tuna from the can. Set each ingredient in single containers, just like a pizza man does. Reserve.

Preheat the oven at 500° F. Spray water in the oven to create humidity.

After the dough has risen the second time, now it is time to transform it into the pizza.

For this operation, you need to free your counter space. Cut the dough in 2 or 3 pieces, depending on how thin you want the crust.

With the rolling pin, roll out and flatten the dough to 1" thickness. Pizza is good when the crust is very thin. Crust is supposed to be a complement to the ingredients, not the main item to taste.

From each small piece of dough, make two small tubes (2 tubes for each pizza) of about ½" in diameter and 12" long. They will be used to divide the pizza in four parts.

Place all the stretched pizza dough on oiled pizza sheets; distribute peeled tomatoes on top of each one as the first layer. Apply on top the tube strips to divide the pizzas in four parts. Bake for the first 15 minutes at 500° F. without any other ingredient. This practice will cook the dough very crispy. Keep the heat at high temperature during the baking time.

Take the pizza out of the oven and place each ingredient in each triangle in the following fashion: basil leaves go at the bottom of each triangle, so it will not burn, then fill one triangle with tuna and olives, one triangle with prosciutto and Mozzarella, the next triangle with preserved artichokes and the fourth triangle with sautéed mushrooms. Drizzle extra-virgin olive oil, season with salt and pepper.

Bake the pizza again for about ten minutes at high temperature.

Tradition of popizze and sgagliozze
(fried puffy dough and fried polenta)

The end of the year, a time to think about the good and not so good things that have happened during the course of the last 12 months, a time to make new goals, a new vision board, a time to be together with all the people you love and celebrate in style, a time to let go of some food restrictions for a few hours and enjoy the gift of food as a token of love. Tomorrow is another day, but today celebrate this passage.

In the South of Italy, we make a dish called Popizze, or Pettole, a type of finger food, nothing but a simple fried puffy dough. The batter mixture of the popizze must rise to double its quantity and must form bubbles on top, which is how to tell it is happy and ready to go. It takes about half hours or just about to rise, it will become a soft, very elastic batter. Make the vegetable oil very hot and spoon in a small quantity of batter at a time, until the space in the oil has been taken and the dough flows freely.

The secret of this dish is to create shapes and forms. When you drop the batter into the hot oil, hold the spoon about 12"-15" above the oil and with a few twists and turns of the spoon make designs with the batter falling in the oil. As the batter hits the oil, it will turn into dough and you will see many different creations come alive that you did not intend to do. You might had a particular shape in mind, let's say a star, a flower, or a hand, but a dog, an angel, or a pen will come out instead.

My grandmother was a master in executing her popizze exactly the way she wanted any shape to be. To control the design, she dipped her hand in the batter, she did not use the spoon and by dropping the dough where and how she wanted in the hot oil, she executed realistic designs. I was never good to execute the design I had in mind, but I am good in making the popizze in any shape they come.

Once the dough is well done and crispy on both sides, take it out of the oil, place it on an absorbent paper to get rid of the excess oil, season each piece to your liking with salt and pepper and serve them warm on a decorative platter. Make a large bunch, they will disappear in a nano second, promise!

If you like them sweet, dust powdered sugar and cinnamon after they have cooled, instead of salt. They are equally delicious and they will look like creations under snow.

In the South of Italy, this is considered a fun finger food made only for Christmas Eve, New Years Eve and Mardi Gras and it was also prepared as street food during respected religious holidays. Today the custom has been revived, along with sgagliozze (fried polenta). In the streets of Bari Vecchia (old Bari), you can still smell miles away popizze and scagliozze being fried in the oil. They are sold in a yellow butcher paper made in a cone, five or seven pieces for one Euro, loaded with salt.

They are so caustic, but so good. The rule is to eat them hot out of the oil, so you can burn the roof of the mouth to prove that you can take them. It is like a test among friends. In winter days, it is a beautiful sensation to get warmed up by a cone or a package of hot fried popizze or scagliozze in your hands and a glass of heavy red wine. After that experience, you might not want to eat for the next three days.

This kind of food is good to do it once a year, together with family and friends. There you have it, you have time until midnight of December 31st to make it and enjoy the moment.

Popizze
(Fried Puffy Dough)
Duration: 60 min.

Ingredients for 6-8 people
8 oz. semola flour
warm water as needed
1 cube of beer yeast
2 teaspoons of honey or white sugar
vegetable oil to fry
salt and black pepper to taste, or powdered sugar and cinnamon

Put all the ingredients in a bowl; add warm water a little at a time to make a dense, velvety batter. Whisk vigorously while poring the water. Cover with a plastic wrap and let it rest for a good rising in a warm area away from ventilation. It will double the size. Cook it as soon as the bubbles appear on top, otherwise if the dough deflates it will not puff up in the hot oil when frying.

Spoon one tablespoon at a time of the batter and drop it in the hot oil. As the batter reaches the hot oil, it will puff up and it will take the most incredible shapes, so make it fun; create the shapes and forms you like.

Fry them until golden and puffy. Drain the excess oil on absorbent paper.

Add salt and black pepper if you want savoury Popizze; add powdered sugar and cinnamon if you want them sweet.

—ɷ—

Sgagliozze
(Fried Polenta Triangles)
Duration: 60 min.

No list of ingredients is necessary for this recipe. Store bought pre-cooked polenta is OK to use. Take it out of the package, slice it in ½″ thick pieces, than fry in hot vegetable oil. Season it with salt and pepper to your liking.

If using the loose corn meal in a package, cook it accordingly to instructions on the box. Transfer the hot polenta on a wooden board to cool, cut it in triangles of about 3″w. x ½″ thick and fry. Season with salt and pepper to your liking.

Sgagliozze

Artichoke Pesto
Duration: 25 min.

Ingredients for 6 people

3 medium size artichokes

5 or 6 cloves of garlic

grated Parmigiano cheese to taste

extra-virgin olive oil as needed to make a creamy mixture

salt and black pepper to taste

1 lb. of basil leaves

a hand full of piñoli (pine nuts)

Prepare a bowl full of acidulated water (it means to add the juice of one lemon and the lemon peels) in which each cleaned artichoke and stems will be placed to prevent discoloration.

Peel the first 2 or 3 layers of the artichokes until leaves appear yellow or lighter green.

Cut about 1″ off the tops to eliminate the spiky tips. Cut off the stems from the artichokes and peel them until the greener fibres are exposed. Split the artichokes in half and cut off the feathery center called the "choke". Keep the artichokes in acidulated water for about fifteen minutes.

I am sure your fingers are now stained from peeling the artichokes, use the same lemon peel to rub your fingers. It works!

Drop the artichokes in a pot with salted boiling water and cook them for about 7 or 8 minutes. Drain the water well.

Brush the artichokes with a bit of olive oil, add salt and pepper and roast them on a hot grill until done, or in an iron skillet over the stove.

To prepare the artichoke pesto:

Roast briefly the pine nuts in a skillet, or cast iron skillet without oil. Please watch them closely, they burn easy. Reserve for later.

Wash the basil and dry it well in a kitchen towel. Place it in a food processor.

Add all the other ingredients in the list to make the artichoke pesto included the roasted artichokes. As for the Parmigiano cheese start with one cup and work your way up, if you like to taste more cheese. Leave piñoli (pine nuts) out of the process, they will be added whole later.

From the top of the food processor, slowly add olive oil while mixing everything together until a creamy and smooth mixture has formed. About 1 or 1-1/2 cup of olive oil will be used. Discard all those artichoke pieces, which did not get processed well.

At the end when the mixture has become a smooth cream, add roasted pine nuts and transfer it to a serving bowl.

Artichokes pesto can be used on pasta, bread or crostini as appetizer, or to stuff the centre of pork chops. Buon appetito!

Note

Any pesto keeps well in the refrigerator for long time as long as it is covered with olive oil.

Chickpeas Cream
Duration: 2 hours if using dry chickpeas
40 min. if using canned chickpeas

Ingredients for 6 people
4 roasted red bell peppers
4 roasted tomatoes
1 roasted garlic head
cooked chickpeas (canned OK)
a hand full of basil leaves
1 or 1-1/2 cup extra-virgin olive oil as needed
salt and pepper to your taste

Cook the chickpeas first; they take longer time to cook, if using the dry kind.

It is OK to use canned pre-cooked chickpeas, but the idea of my healthy cuisine is to make every food fresh.

Bake bell peppers, tomatoes and garlic at the same time, in separate baking vessels as follows:

To roast bell peppers, you can either scorch over open flame, grill, or bake them in the oven at 400° F for about 20 minutes, or until all the sides are scorched. Turn them over every so often while baking.

Cut tomatoes in half, drizzle olive oil over, season with salt and pepper and bake at 400° F for about 20 minutes, or until they look soft.

Place the garlic head in aluminium foil, or in the garlic clay pot baker, don't peel it, cut the top off, drizzle olive oil, season with salt and pepper to your liking. Close the foil and bake for 10-15 minutes at 400° F.

It is time to assemble the ingredients after they are all baked.

Drain the water from the chickpeas, take the garlic pulp out of the shells, place all the ingredients at once in the food processor, included olive oil, salt and pepper, except basil leaves. Blend well into a smooth cream.

Place the chickpeas cream in a bowl and decorate it with chopped basil leaves, add coarsely ground black pepper, or hot chili pepper, as you like.

Note

Chickpeas cream can be used as a dip, or spread on meats, or even mixed with rice or pasta (in this case a cup of the pasta cooking water needs to be added in the mixture).

Cucumber Compote
Duration: 10 min.

Ingredients for 6 people

2 cucumbers coarsely chopped
2 tablespoons of stone ground mustard
4 or 5 anchovies in olive oil
2 shallots
red hot pepper (as liked)
a hand full of Italian parsley and basil

2 tablespoons of green olives
2 teaspoons of capers
3 or 4 cloves of garlic
2 tablespoons of olive oil
the juice of one lime

Peel the cucumbers, split them in half and take the seeds out with a small spoon.

Put all the ingredients in the food processor, except capers and mix until they become creamy.

Transfer the creamy compote into a serving bowl and top it with a hand full of capers. Add a few drops of olive oil if it looks a bit dry. Adjust the seasoning to your liking.

This is a perfect dip to eat with raw vegetables. Otherwise it can be spread on grilled steak, on steamed fish.

—⚋—

Anchovies Paste
Duration: 10 min.

Ingredients for 6-8 people

2 garlic cloves
4 or 5 sun dried tomatoes
1 can of anchovies
4 or 5 tablespoons of black olives

3.5 oz. of goat cheese
a few leaves of basil and Italian parsley
hot pepper to taste
olive oil enough to emulsify

Blend all the ingredients together in the food processor. From the top of the machine pour olive oil slowly to emulsify until the ingredients become creamy.

Use it as a dip, or spread it on baguette bread slices, on meats and fish dishes.

Mediterranean Salad Dressing
Duration: 10 min.

Ingredients for 6 people
1 cucumber
2 leeks
a hand full of mint leaves
extra-virgin olive oil to make the emulsion
salt and black pepper to your taste

Cut the cucumber in half; take out the seeds from the centre. Chop the cucumber and leeks in chunks. Place all the ingredients in the food processor and while the machine is going on slow setting, slowly add olive oil from the top of the food processor to make a smooth creamy emulsion, about 1 or 1-1/2 cup of oil will be used, depending on how dense you like it to be.

Take it out and pour it over any salad.

This creamy dressing must be consumed the same day it is made, cannot be kept in the refrigerator.

—◆—

Vinaigrette Dressing
Duration: 10 min.

Ingredients for 6 people
2 garlic cloves
2 ginger slices
2 teaspoons of any mustard
2 or 3 tablespoons of balsamic vinegar
½ cup of olive oil
salt and black pepper granulated course

Finely chop garlic and ginger. Place all the ingredients in a glass jar with a lid, close it and firmly shake the jar, until a creamy dressing has formed. This dressing can be kept in the refrigerator for a few days, but why bother, it is so easy and fast to make that it can be done on the spot every time and served fresh. Ginger is not a spice used in Italian cuisine, I use it sometimes to add more character to simple recipes.

Parsley And Cilantro Salsa
Duration: 10 min.

Ingredients for 6 people

2 oz. of toasted almonds
1 head of roasted garlic
1 bunch of cilantro
1 bunch of Italian parsley

juice of 2 limes
extra-virgin olive oil to make the emulsion
salt and black pepper to taste

Toast the almonds first at 400° F for about 10 minutes. Reserve.

Wash parsley and cilantro. Reserve.

To toast the garlic, place it on the aluminium foil, cut the top off, but don't peel it, drizzle olive oil over, season with salt and pepper, close the foil and bake it at 400° F. for about 10-15 minutes. Take it out of the foil and squeeze the garlic pulp out of its skins.

In the food processor, mix all the ingredients at once. From the top of the machine, slowly pour olive oil to make a smooth emulsion and turn the ingredients into a salsa.

—⟋⟍—

Green Bell Pepper Salsa
Duration: 30 min.

Ingredients for 6 people

2 green bell peppers
2 garlic cloves
1 bunch of cilantro

2 slices of stale bread
1 cup of extra-virgin olive oil
salt and pepper to your taste

Roast the green bell peppers in the oven at 400° F for about 20 minutes, or scorch them over open flame. As soon as they are manageable, take the skin off.

Place all the ingredients in the food processor; slowly pour olive oil from the top of the machine to emulsify. Blend until the ingredients become a creamy mixture. The mixture must be smooth, add more oil, if it looks thick.

Parsley can be substituted if cilantro is not of your taste.

This creamy mixture can be used in a variety of ways:

on hamburgers and sandwiches – on grilled pork chops – in beans soup – with short pasta (in this case a bit of a pasta cooking water needs to be added).

It is super!

Dry Rub For Ribs
Duration: 10 min.

Ingredients for 6 people

1 onion finely chopped

1 lemon peel Julienne cut (very thin strips)

0.5 oz. of brown sugar

3 or 4 slices of ginger grated

salt to your liking

1 garlic head finely chopped

1 oz. of coriander seed crushed

crushed dry chili pepper to your taste

zest of 1 lime

To crush all these spices to a fine powder, use either the small food processor intended for spices, or marble pestle and mortar. Scorch the dry chili peppers over open flame, mix it with the ingredients. Add more chili pepper, if you like the rub to be spicy.

Put it on the meat to be grilled, rub and massage the meat vigorously.

Let it rest for about thirty minutes, and then grill it.

—∽—

Salsa Marinara For Ribs
Duration: 15 min.

Ingredients for 6 people

4 or 5 garlic cloves

a hand full of Italian parsley

1 medium can of tomato sauce

olive oil

1 small red onion

½ cup of orange juice

grated nutmeg

2 teaspoons of coffee ground

Chop all the ingredients, sauté onion and garlic together in olive oil, add the orange juice and let it evaporate for a few minutes. Add tomato sauce and the rest of the ingredients. Simmer covered at a slow heat for about 20 minutes.

Serve either warm or room temperature with grilled meats, grilled shrimps and any raw fish appetizers. It can be used as a sauce for a pasta plate (add a cup of the pasta cooking water while simmering).

Salamora
Duration: 10 min.

Ingredients for 4 people
2 garlic heads
peel of 2 oranges
salt and colour peppercorn to taste
1-1/2 cup of extra-virgin olive oil

Chop garlic really fine, Julienne the peel of two oranges, season with salt and pepper to your liking. Place all the ingredients in a glass jar with olive oil, close the lid and shake well. Pour it over a salad, or over grilled meats and fish, or over white steamed rice. This is a simple solution deriving from Ancona area (central Italy) and it is another way to use all the oranges from your tree.

—⁓—

Garlic Paste
Duration: 10 min.

Ingredients for 6 people
7 garlic heads
6 or 7 ginger slices
salt and black pepper to your liking
extra-virgin olive oil to make the emulsion

To fill up a glass jar of barely 2 oz. you need to use at least 7 garlic heads. More people, more ingredients.

Place all the ingredients in the food processor and while the machine is going on slow setting, slowly add olive oil from the top of the food processor to make a smooth creamy emulsion, about 1 or 1-1/2 cup of oil will be used, depending on how dense you like it to be.

Take it out and pour it inside of a glass jar hermetically closed with a lid to keep in the refrigerator for a variety of uses:

on bruschetta – in sandwiches – on grilled meat and fish, in any roast, to start any sauce.
This is heaven!

How to conserve home made sauces
(a Pasteurization process)

All of the sauces listed in these last few chapters came from my family.

The sauces were made either as a trial, or just because my family never bought anything prepared and processed by the food industry. We always made our own sauces, our own fresh pasta simple or stuffed and a variety of conserved food. We made large quantities to keep for the winter, or to surprise guests when they invited themselves at the last minute. It was much less expensive to make and keep them for months and so much healthier than the store bought products.

I could not include in this book all of my family's production, perhaps it will the subject for another book.

Bear in mind that any sauce, or cream can be made to conserve.

After all the ingredients have been processed into a sauce or a cream, to keep them stored in the kitchen pantry, they must be pasteurized. The process is really easy; it is done in only a few hours. Wash all the glass mason jars with their lids needed for the quantity of cream and sauces you are making.

Fill them with home made sauces or creams. Close the lids very tight.

On the bottom of the stock pot place 3 or 4 thick kitchen towels to protect the glass mason jars from breaking with the heat of the fire.

Place in the pot all the filled mason jars; align them on the bottom and stack on top of each other. Fill up the pot with water to cover all the jars completely.

Turn the fire on at medium speed. Cover the pot with the lid and start the process of pasteurization, which will last for 45 minutes. Let them stand in the water until cooled; it will be easier to take the jars out of the pot. Dry the water and store them in the kitchen pantry away from heat sources.

Perhaps one or two jars will break, not to worry. This happens when the glass has a bubble in it and it was not corrected during the manufacturing process.

Create yourself a really great fun in making these home made sauces.

Invite people and make them together. Buon divertimento!

Preserved Specialties For The Winter

Coffee Cheese Cake
Duration: 60 min.

Ingredients for 6 people
2 packs (10-14 oz. max.) of any chocolate cookies crumbled
4 oz. of melted butter
a pinch of salt

Filling
2 packs of any cream cheese
9 oz. of sugar
3 whole eggs
5 oz. of milk (low fat OK)
4 teaspoons of vanilla
2 cups of sweetened espresso coffee (demi-tasse size)
2 oz. of warm water
nutmeg to decorate

Preheat the oven at 350° F.

Grease very lightly and flour the baking pan to use. Good to use a collapsible baking pan.

Crumble almost into powder all the chocolate cookies. Add melted butter and salt. Mix well and press this mixture to cover the bottom of the pan up against the walls of the pan about ½" high.

In the food processor mix all the cheese and the sugar to form a smooth cream.

Add to this cream one egg at the time, vanilla, two cups of espresso room temperature, milk and water. Mix well until a foamy, light cream is obtained.

Transfer the cream to the baking pan, on top of the crumbled cookies. Move the pan up and down on the table to get rid of all the air bubbles.

Bake for about 40-45 minutes (some oven cook differently than others), or until the toothpick test comes out clean. Let it cool down.

Decorate with grated nutmeg and powdered sugar if you like.

It can be refrigerated.

It is always a great success!

Coffee Cheese Cake

Croccantino
(Crunchy Tart)
Duration: 45 min.

Ingredients for 4 to 6 people

3 whole eggs   ½ cup of sugar

lemon zest   pine nuts (piñoli) to your liking to fill the piecrust

a few drops of amaretto liqueur (if not available use vanilla)

To make the tart crust

1 cup of flour   2/3 of a butter stick, or a margarine stick

3 tablespoons of water   2 teaspoons of brown sugar

a pinch of salt

Make the tart crust first. **All the ingredients for the crust must be very cold!**

Mix all the ingredients until the butter is crumbled. Use a fork to mix, or better the hand held Cuisipro Pastry Blender. This device has six sturdy blades and an oversized handle for superior performance when blending butter or margarine into dry ingredients.

Add three tablespoons of water and work the dough very briefly with your hands. Try not to overwork the ingredients, otherwise the heat of your hands will cause the butter to warm up and the dough to fall apart.

The dough must have a soft consistency. Place it in the refrigerator covered in a plastic wrap for about half hour to keep it cold. It will be easy to roll it out later.

Warm up the oven at 355° F.

With the rolling pan, stretch the dough to the size of the baking pan you are using. I make my Croccantino in a rectangular shape pan with a collapsible bottom, size 14" x 4.5", just to give a different shape to this tart.

For the first part of the baking, puncture the dough with a fork, then cover it with aluminium foil and fill up the centre with dry beans. Blind baking doesn't create bubbles in the dough and will make a crispy crust. Bake for about 15 minutes. The dough must be almost golden.

Beat the eggs and mix in the rest of the ingredients, which will be the filling of the tart.

Fill up the tart crust evenly. Bake at 355° F., for about 20-28 minutes, until the eggs are coagulated. Cover only the edges of the tart with aluminium foil to avoid burning the crust. Take the foil out during the last ten minutes of the baking to allow the edges of the crust to brown in a golden colour.

The filling must be moist on top, but after cooling, it will firm up.

Decorated with edible flowers, like nasturtium.

Croccantino with the same ingredients and same procedure can be made also in many tartlets of one portion per person.

Croccantino

Strawberry Cheese Cake
Duration: 60 min.

Ingredients for 4 to 6 people
2/3 cup of crushed chocolate cookies (12 to 13 cookies)
finely grated orange peel
2 tablespoons of melted butter
3 packages of 8-oz. cream cheese (low fat OK)
¾ cup of sugar
2 tablespoons of all-purpose flour
3 whole eggs beaten
1¾ cup of strawberries
¼ cup of strawberry juice
¼ cup of fat-free milk

Preheat oven to 375° F. Cut strawberries in very small pieces. In a blender puree ¼ cup of strawberries, strain the seeds. Set aside.

To make the crust, combine in a bowl crushed cookies and grated orange peel in the quantity you like. Stir in butter and mix well. Press crust on the bottom of a 9" collapsible bottom pan and set aside.

In a mixing bowl beat cream cheese, milk, sugar and flour with the mixer on medium speed for about five minutes. Mix in eggs and more grated orange peel until well combined.

Fold in strawberries whole, strawberry jiuce and the strained strawberry puree. Pour into the pan previously lined with the chocolate cookies crust.

Bake 35 to 40 minutes or until around the edges appears set when gently shaken and the toothpick test comes out clean.

Cool for 30 minutes. Using a small sharp knife, loosen edges from sides of pan. Remove the pan. Cool completely.

Cover with a glass dome or aluminium foil and refrigerate at least 4 hours before serving.

Mont Blanc
(Chocolate Cake Without Flour)
Duration: 20 min.

Ingredients for 4 to 6 people

1 or 2 lb. of chestnuts depending on number of people

1 cup of unsweetened dark cacao powder

sugar to your liking

pre-made whipped cream OK

Peel the outer shells of the chestnuts.

Boil all the chestnuts in water. Peel the thin skin.

Crush all the boiled chestnuts on a windmill (not in the food processor, otherwise you have a mushy pulp as a result).

Mix dark cacao powder into the chestnuts with the sugar in the amount best suited to your palate. Adjust to taste.

Place the chestnuts onto a serving platter in a mountain shape; cover the top with whipped cream, as if it were snow. Done.

This recipe comes from the city of Torino in the North of Italy bordering with France, that's why the name resents of a French influence. In Italian is called "Monte Bianco".

—❦—

Chocolate Torte
(Another Version Without Flour)
Duration: 60 min.

Ingredients for 4 to 6 people

8 oz. of bittersweet chocolate cut into small pieces

4 oz. of unsalted butter cut into small pieces

zest of 1 orange

2/3 cup sugar

5 large eggs separated

1 oz. of raw almonds chopped

pinch of salt

Preheat oven to 325° degrees F. Butter and flour the base of a 10" round cake pan.

Combine chocolate and butter in a bain-marie or in a bowl over simmering water.

Whisk together the egg yolks and all but 3 tablespoons of the sugar.

Stir melted chocolate into egg yolks until thoroughly combined.

With an electric mixer, on medium speed, beat egg whites and salt until a soft peak forms. Gradually beat in the remaining sugar and continue to whip until egg whites are stiff but not dry. Add chopped almonds and orange zest.

Carefully fold chocolate mixture into egg whites. Pour the mixture into prepared pan.

Bake for about 45 minutes. Turn the torte out onto a rack immediately.

As the torte cools, the centre will sink and crack - do not worry.

Chocolate Torte Without Flour

Chocolate: food for the Gods, good for me

Cacao bean is the purest form of chocolate, "food for the Gods".

Cacao is one of nature's most nutritious foods, due to its wide array of unique properties. It is the number one source of magnesium, high in sulphur, which is the "mineral of beauty", rich in antioxidants, it is a natural anti-depressant, and an aphrodisiac!

There has been a long time association to chocolate and love. Inside of Perugina's classic Baci Chocolate (Baci means "kisses" in Italian) there is a love message included in the silver wrapper of the small chocolate bite looking like a breast of a woman with a nipple.

The fascination of chocolate being associated with passion and love, probably came from movies in the '30s projecting the protagonists as " les femmes fatales", sensual, blonde, bejewelled hands, always smoking a cigarette with a cigarette holder, eating a box of chocolates in bed dressed with silk sheets. No wonder women crave chocolate! It tastes divine and it makes us feel like a femme fatale too!

Not too fast. Actually, there is no prove that chocolate is an aphrodisiac and it is not so pure either. Chocolate as a finished product is usually mixed with high sugar content, hydrogenated fats and dairy products. Indulge but don't overdue.

Roasted cacao beans contain subtle amounts of caffeine that when boiled in water turn into a stimulant for the nervous system similar to a coffee drink and accelerate the pulse, but when cacao beans (seeds) are not roasted and boiled in water that stimulant effect is not noticeable.

Cacao is a small evergreen tree native to the lower eastern part of the Andes in South America. Cacao grows in partial shade at very low elevations between 20 degrees North and South latitude, in a temperature between 25° and 35° C (77-95 F°). Cacao tree loves precipitation up to three meters (10 ft.).

Archeologists tell us that the Olmecs, the oldest civilization of the Americas (1500-400 BC), were probably the first users of cacao, followed by other Mesoamerican (Central American) peoples like the Mayans (600 BC) and then the Aztecs (400 AD).

Cacao was their symbol of abundance. It was used in religious rituals dedicated to Quetzalcoatl, the Aztec God who brought cocoa tree to man, as the legend says. Cacao was also offered to Chak ek Chuah, the Mayan patron saint of cocoa and as an offering at the funerals of noblemen. It was also important as a currency and has been used as such, in certain parts of South America, right up to the beginning of the 20th century.

Mayans and Aztecs mostly used cacao seeds as a drink with the addition of maize and vanilla, or a sauce (Mole) with ground chili peppers.

The legendary Spanish Conquistador Hernán Cortés who caused the fall of the Aztec Empire, in 1528, carried back from Mexico the cacao seeds to Spain, making the Spanish court fall under the spell of this exotic elixir. The wealthy Spaniards mixed cacao beans powder with sugar and vanilla, or cinnamon, turning it into the fashionable drink of the élite.

Chocolate didn't arrive in the rich Italian region of Tuscany until the start of the 17th century and took almost fifty years to become popular. Under the Florentine De' Medici dynasty chocolate was used as a means of public relations. The De' Medici family exploited chocolate to gain influence or favours in the very same way they used art and architecture to enhance their prestige and power in Renaissance Tuscany.

To successfully compete with the chocolate used by the Spaniards, the De' Medici family commissioned the development of new chocolate recipes resulting in a wide variety of novelties especially using musk and jasmine-flavoured chocolate. The De' Medici family's recipes became state secrets and were served to local and foreign dignitaries to further prove their magnificence.

Continue

Hot chocolate was a pretty hot commodity in the French courts too. It was served at the wedding of Louis XIII and Anne of Austria in 1615 and flowed freely at the buffets of Louis XIV in Versailles.

Later in the 17th century Portuguese brought the cacao seeds to West Africa and started a new cultivation in those parts. Today most of the world production of cacao comes from Nigeria, Ghana, Ivory Coast, and Cameroon.

Despite the cocoa bean originating in the 'New World', chocolate arrived in North America much later. The chocolate drink was first introduced in 1765 when John Hanau brought cocoa beans from the West Indies into Massachusetts.

Ghirardelli chocolate's history dates back to California's gold rush. Domenico Ghirardelli, a native of Rapallo, Italy, living in Lima, Peru, was the owner of a successful confectionery business at a young age of 31 years old. Domenico had heard of the fabulous riches in gold being found in California, and in 1849 he sailed to California with the intention of striking it rich and to go back to Peru with his new fortune. But his plans took a different direction and after many business adventures and the San Francisco fire in 1851 that destroyed many surrounding cities and businesses, Domenico bought out his business partner, opened a new business and renamed it "Mrs. Ghirardelli & Company." By 1853 and the advent of the industrial revolution, chocolate and cacao in United States was no longer a precious elixir destined to the wealthy, but it was made popular for everybody to enjoy.

In Florence, Italy, the slow food movement organizes every year a variety of chocolate shows and fairs to promote artisans with their chocolate art, which has always been an important feature in Italian food tradition.

Photograph:
White's Chocolate House, London c.1708 coloured lithograph published by Cadbury.
Note: Not a contemporary 1708 illustration (late 19th-century at earliest).
Public domain photograph expired copyright.

Marbleized Cake
Duration: 95 min.

Ingredients for 4 to 6 people
7 oz. of white sugar
6 oz. of unsalted butter
3 whole eggs
7 oz. of white flour
3 teaspoons of baking powder
peel of 1 lemon grated
2 oz. of cacao powder
½ cup of milk
powdered sugar

Preheat oven at 350° F. Use the food processor if you like to mix all the ingredients.

Mix butter, sugar and 3 whole eggs, one at the time, to make a creamy substance.

Add flour slowly. Mix well for about 5 minutes.

Incorporate baking powder and grated lemon peel.

Melt the cacao in the milk over a double boiler. Make it really silky. Reserve.

Keep the two mixtures separate for right now.

Lightly smear a baking pan with butter and dust it with flour.

In the baking pan drop alternatively, one batter of one colour on top of the other of different colour; practically a spoon of the white mixture and a spoon of the brown mixture.

To obtain a marbleizing effect, do not mix the two colours. Continue to do so until the two mixtures are used up.

To eliminate bubbles into the mixture, tap a few times the baking pan on the surface you are working on.

Place it in the oven for about one hour. To test it for doneness dip a toothpick in the middle, if it comes out clean, the cake is done.

Cool the cake and sprinkle it with powdered sugar.

This is not a very sweet cake, but excellent with cappuccino, or espresso coffee.

Chocolate Tart
Duration: 40 min.

Ingredients for 4 to 6 people
3.5 oz. of dark unsweetened chocolate
¼ cup of whipped cream
1.7 oz. of chopped almonds
2 tablespoons of Grand Marnier

To make the pâte brisée (pie crust)
1 cup of flour
2/3 of a butter stick, or a margarine stick
3 tablespoons of water
2 teaspoons of brown sugar
a pinch of salt

Make the pâte brisée first. **All the ingredients for the crust must be very cold!**

Mix all the ingredients to breadcrumbs consistency. Use a fork to mix, or better the hand held Cuisipro Pastry Blender. This device has six sturdy blades and an oversized handle for superior performance when blending butter or margarine into dry ingredients.

Add three tablespoons of water and work the dough very briefly with your hands. Try not to overwork the ingredients, otherwise the heat of your hands will cause the butter to warm up and the dough to fall apart.

The dough must have a soft consistency. Place it in the refrigerator for about half hour to keep it cold, it will be easier to roll it out later.

Pre-heat the oven at 355° F.

With the rolling pan, stretch the dough to the size of the baking pan you are using. It is better to use a pan with a collapsible bottom, it is easy to unfold it when serving.

For the first part of the baking, puncture the dough with a fork, then cover it with aluminium foil and fill up the centre with dry beans. Blind baking doesn't create bubbles in the dough and will make a crispy crust.

Bake for about 20 minutes. Ovens cook differently from one brand to another. After this time check with a toothpick, if the dough is still soft, remove the aluminium foil and continue to bake until the dough is golden/brown.

Cool it down.

In a double boiler melt chocolate and butter into a silky cream. Mix in whipped cream and Grand Marnier. Fold gently with a soft cake spatula.

Pour the chocolate mixture onto the pâte brisée and cover with chopped almonds. Serve it cool, or room temperature.

Custom and traditions of a Christmas dinner

In Italy, in the province of Pavia, Christmas Eve dinner starts with a soup of lasagna mixed with mushrooms sauté in oil and garlic. In old times in Italy newborn babies were wrapped in bands of white cloth to keep their tender legs very straight and prevent them from growing bowed. In the fantasy of the local people this dish represents those bands, therefore it is made in honour of baby Jesus being born on Christmas Eve.

Many specialties follow this first dish: marinated eel, salted stockfish and escargot.

The small horns of the escargot allude to discord and disagreement between people, therefore they need to be hidden in the stomach of the guests to properly prepare themselves to a peaceful Christmas, as the legend says.

Other fundamental specialties are risotto cooked in any style, roasted turkey, boiled capon dressed with mustard. In the same province of Pavia, going more toward the inland towns and villages, included in the typical menu of the holidays, after a risotto plate, there are stuffed onions with meat and focaccia bread.

A must have dessert for the end of the dinner is the Sbrisolona Torte, a typical dessert of that area. It is a crisp and friable torte, which accompanies Torrone, Panettone and Pâte Brisee' all hand made and found in each home. The Sbrisolona Torte doesn't really mark the end of the dinner, there are still all the fruits of the season parading on the table: citrus, grapes and dry nuts. Apples, even though are fruits of the Christmas season, they are not eaten because they represent the fruit with which Adam and Eve committed the original sin.

Women bake hand made breads for Christmas holidays. The portion to use for every meal is cut and reserved, then all Christmas breads are placed on the table and everyone in turn must take a piece every day from Christmas Eve until the 31st of December.

It is believed that Christmas breads do not go bad, do not grow mould and therefore they are good to cure bellyache.

Sbrisolona Torte

Torta Sbrisolona
(Crisp And Friable Torte)
Duration: 50 min.

Ingredients for 4 to 6 people
7 oz. of raw almonds
7 oz. of white flour
7 oz. of wheat flour, or corn flour
2 egg yokes
7 oz. of brown sugar
0.6 oz. of baking powder
2 or 3 teaspoons of vanilla
grated peel of 1 lemon
7 oz. of butter
powdered sugar
butter and flour to line the pan

Chop finely all the almonds; place them in a bowl with all the ingredients and butter cut in chunks.

Work the ingredients into a dough, but don't overwork it. The dough must be soft and have some small lumps.

Place the lumpy dough in the baking pan, previously buttered and floured.

Bake at 350-355° F. for about 40-45 minutes, until the top will appear well golden and crispy.

When done, let it cool down; sprinkle powdered sugar on top.

This torte comes from the region of Lombardy, in the North of Italy.

Wine:
The right wine to match with Torta Sbrisolona is Moscato Oltrepo' Pavese, or White Greco.

Lucrezia Borgia's Wedding Cake – Circa 1502
Duration: 45 min.

Ingredients for 4 to 6 people
1 pack of sugar cookie crust or any biscotti well crumbled
1 stick of butter
2 tablespoons of melted butter
2 cups of almonds previously roasted
1 cup of sugar
3 egg whites
1 pack of spaghetti pasta

Lightly grease a 10" pan. Crumble the cookies and add melted butter to let the crumbles stick together. Fill the bottom of the pan with sugar cookie crumbles, making sure to press firmly against the walls of the pan, up to ½" high.

Any biscotti will serve the same purpose, but they must be well crumbled.

Partially cook the spaghetti in salted water for only 4-5 minutes and reserve. They will be cooking more in the baking process.

Melt the butter and reserve.

Beat the egg whites; mix in sugar, butter and almonds. Pour half of this mixture on the sugar cookie crust. Add half of the cooked spaghetti.

Make a second layer with the rest of the mixture and the rest of the spaghetti.

Spoon on top a little more of melted butter. Cover with the coarsely chopped almonds. Bake at 350° until golden brown.

Sprinkle powdered sugar on top if desired.

The spaghetti in this torte symbolizes the golden hair of Lucrezia Borgia who invented it for her own wedding day.

Historical Note
Lucrezia Borgia was born during Italy's Renaissance period (1320–1520), a time when Italian artists, architects, and scientists rose to world appreciation. She was born into one of the most well known families in world history: the Borgias, who sought to control as much of Italy as they could.

Lucrezia Borgia, Duchess of Ferrara, earned a reputation as a political schemer in fifteenth century Italy. In actuality, she was simply used by her father and brothers to further their own political goals.

Lucrezia Borgia

Almond Soft Cake

Duration: 2 hrs. for rising
1 hr. for baking

Ingredients for 8 people

17.5 oz. of all-purpose flour
3.5 oz. of raisins
3.5 oz. of almonds peeled
2 oz. of brown sugar
2.5 of butter
1.7 oz. of milk (low fat OK)
1.5 oz. of beer yeast
5 oz. of water
½ cup of rum
a pinch of salt
powdered sugar

To peel the almonds, drop them in boiling water and parboil for only 4-5 minutes. Transfer in a kitchen towel and rub them together to loosen the skin.

Chop the almonds medium fine; place the raisins in the rum to soak for 15 minutes; melt the butter.

Set everything aside.

Warm up the milk and dissolve the beer yeast in it.

Squeeze very strongly the raisins to eliminate all the rum, otherwise the rum will react against the yeast and will prevent the dough from rising. In the food processor place flour, a pinch of salt, water and all the ingredients at once.

At medium speed work the ingredients into medium soft dough.

Place the dough in a large bowl, cover with a plastic film and let it rise away from wind draft for about an hour. After this time, rework the dough on a flat surface by push down the air.

Divide the dough in a couple of pieces and shape it to the baking pans you are going to use, make a few cuts on top with a blade or a very sharp knife.

Lightly oil and flour the baking pans, place the dough in them to rise again for another hour.

Brush an egg wash (egg white beaten with 2 teaspoons of water) over the risen dough and bake at 375° F. for about an hour, or until the toothpick test comes out clean.

Sprinkle powdered sugar on top after it has cooled.

Scarcella – A Traditional Easter Cake
Duration: 60 min.

Ingredients for 4 to 6 people

35 oz. of white flour	4 oz. of butter or olive oil
10.5 oz. of sugar	0.4 oz of baking powder or 3 teaspoons
17 fluid oz. of warm milk	3 or 4 whole raw eggs for decoration
7 or 8 whole eggs	1 egg white (for egg wash)
vanilla to taste	coloured pralines
1 pinch of salt	chopped lemon rinds

Preheat oven at 350° F.

Mix all the ingredients well. Use milk as a thinning liquid for the mixture. Mixture must be soft, but not runny.

Knead the mixture into a soft ball. Let it rest for about 1 hr. covered with a plastic film and a kitchen cloth over. After rising time, cut a small piece of dough and reserve, it will be used later to make strips of decorations; start forming the shape of your liking.

Be creative with the dough. For instance in Puglia, we make a doll, or a vase, or an angel, or a heart. To help your creativity you may use any kind of mould, or any pan shaped in a certain design available in your kitchen.

After your design is formed, gently push 3 raw eggs not cracked in various places of the Scarcella dough most pleasing to your eyes, push the eggs firmly into the dough.

With the small piece of dough previously reserved, make 6 strips of about 3-1/2″ in length and 3/8″ wide.

Crisscross the strips over each egg; paint a little egg wash on the bottom side of the strips and stick them on the dough. This way the eggs will be strapped and secure during baking. To make an egg wash use only the albumen (white of the egg), with two teaspoons of water mixed in. Brush it all over on the Scarcella too.

Add the coloured pralines in the quantity you like.

Rest it in the baking pan for about 30 minutes.

Place the Scarcella on a lightly greased baking sheet and bake it for about 30 minutes at 350° F. until golden brown on top. Let it cool.

This is considered a sweet type of bread, not really a cake. Eat it alone, or dip it into coffee, or cappuccino, as we do in Puglia. Eat the eggs too, they are now baked and only good for a couple of days. Keep it covered with a plastic wrap. Do not refrigerate it!

Cultural Note

Scarcella is an Easter specialty and it is not made any other time of the year.

American kids hunts their coloured Easter eggs, Italian kids and women, in the week between Palm Sunday and Easter Sunday will receive one Scarcella per person by another member of the family. The eggs, which by the time Scarcella is baked will be hard boiled, symbolize the rebirth of Christ on Easter and women's fertility.

There you have it. Another religious and cultural bread/cake in which lot of history and symbolism are held. It is a common sweet in the south of Italy.

Scarcella

Baked Apples
Duration: 20 min.

Ingredients for 4 people
a hand full of unsalted walnuts
apples as many as you like
2-1/2 cups of orange juice

Grand Marnier
white or brown sugar to your liking
grated, or julienne orange peels

Crack as many walnuts as you wish and roast them in the oven a 350° F. for less than 10 minutes. Coarsely chop them and set aside.

Slice lengthwise as many apples as you like about 1-1/2" thick.

Place all the sliced apples in a baking dish; cover them with 2 cups of orange juice.

Drizzle Grand Marnier over, sprinkle white or brown sugar to your liking and add grated, or julienne orange peels. Use only the thin layer of the exterior skin of the orange, not the white spongy part, it is bitter.

Bake the apples for about 10 minutes. For this recipe, apples can also be cooked on the stove for about the same time. The apples must not be overcooked.

Before serving add the chopped walnuts. Serve warm as is, or let the apples cool down and add them to any ice cream of your liking.

Spirits: Accompany with a glass of Grand Marnier, or Muscat from Sicily, or Prosecco.

—m—

Cooked Peaches In Wine
Duration: 20 min.

Ingredients for 4 people
2 or 3 half peaches per person
brown sugar
any edible flower for colour and decoration

Amaretti cookies
whipped cream
2-1/2 cups of red house wine

Peeled all the peaches, cut them in half and place centre down in a baking pan.

Sprinkle brown sugar; cover the peaches with house red wine and bake for about 10-12 minutes at 375° F.

When done, transfer 2 or 3 half peaches into each plate, centre up. Crumble the Amaretti cookies and fill the centre of each peach. The cooked wine has become light syrup, add it to the peaches. Top with whipped cream.

Use some edible flowers like nasturtiums to decorate. They taste really good, whether they are fresh or candied. Serve the peaches warm, or room temperature.

This recipe comes from the Northern Italian region of Piedmont and it is called:
"Pesche alla Piemontese".

Pastiera Napoletana

Pastiera Napoletana
(Naples Style Ricotta Pie)
Duration: 90 min.

Ingredients for 6 to 8 people
17.5 oz. of flour
7 oz. of sugar
7 oz. of butter
2 whole eggs
1 teaspoon of baking powder
milk enough to mix

Make the base dough first with the ingredients listed at the top. Mix all the ingredients using milk as the wet ingredient. Use milk a little at a time while mixing until all the ingredients come together in a soft ball. Rest the dough covered with a plastic film while preparing the ingredients.

Ingredients for the pie filling
8 oz. of pearl barley
17.5 oz. of ricotta cheese
12.5 oz. of sugar
6 egg yokes
cinnamon to your liking
grated peel of 1 lemon or orange

Cook the pearl barley in salted boiling water, just like you would cook pasta, but pearl barley needs to be cooked thoroughly and not al dente. Drain the water.

Place the cooked barley in a large mixing bowl, crack the eggs, use the yokes now and reserve the albumen (white part of the eggs); add all the other ingredients for the filling. Mix uniformly.

Beat the white of the eggs to a foam. If a hard peak has formed, you know the foam is ready. Fold the egg whites in the rest of the ingredients.

From the dough made previously, cut a small piece. Out of this piece cut many strips of 1" wide, 10" long.

Preheat the oven at 375° F.

Shape the dough in a 10" baking pan. It is better to use a pan with holes at the bottom, which allows the dough to cook thoroughly.

Fill the dough with the mixture. Tap the pan on the table a few times to get rid of bubbles inside the mixture.

Place the strips of dough in a crisscross fashion over the mixture. Brush some egg wash over the strips and around the edge, or a small amount of melted butter.

Bake for about 1 hour or until the toothpick test comes out clean and the top is golden brown.

Cartellate
(Christmas Sweets)

32 oz. of white flour
7 oz. of olive oil
5 oz. of dry white wine or as needed
vanilla to taste
grated peel of 1 lemon
vegetable oil to fry

On a wooden surface, or on a counter top spread white flour, make a well and place all the ingredients in the centre. With a fork work your way from the centre out until all the flour has been mixed with the ingredients.

Work the dough with strength, it must turn out a smooth and hard dough.

Cut the dough in smaller pieces to make it more manageable and keep the rest under plastic wrap to avoid hardening.

Flour your surface and with a rolling pan spread the first piece of dough to make a very thin layer of about 1/8" in thickness.

With a scalloped wheel cut this thin layer of dough into many strips of about 1" in width.

Roll each strip on itself clockwise not too tight to form a rosette. Make a few turns to obtain a 3" diameter. Pinch the dough a few times in crucial areas of the rosette to make it stay together when you will fry it. Continue until all the dough is exhausted.

In a skillet fry the rosettes in plenty vegetable oil. Do not crowd the pan. Cartellate must have a light golden color. Drain the excess of oil on absorbent paper. Cool them down.

At this point you can choose to dust powdered sugar, or to immerse them in what is called "Vino Cotto" cooked wine made with fresh figs. I have included Vino Cotto recipe, but you can also purchase a bottle in gourmet Italian stores. Price is generally high, because it takes many, many pounds of fresh figs to make a small bottle.

Cartellate

Vino Cotto
(Cooked Wine From Fresh Figs)

To make a bottle of 33.8 fluid oz.
8.5 lb. of any fresh figs are needed

Fill up with water a tall and large pot, place in it the 8.5 lb. of fresh figs skin on and bring them to a boil for a couple of hours at low heat. Stir occasionally.

After this time prepare a second large pot. With the help of a strainer with a tight net, filter the water from the first pot, making sure all fig seeds remain in the strainer. Leave the cooked figs in the first pot.

Boil only the filtered water for 2 hours more at medium low heat. Stir occasionally.

Prepare a third pot. Filter again this fig water, which by now has been boiling for 4 hours, making sure all fig seeds remain in the strainer again.

Meanwhile cover with fresh water the 8.5 lb. of figs that you had in the first pot when you started this process. Boil the figs again for 2 more hours.

Stir occasionally.

At this point you will have 2 pots on the stove boiling: one pot with water which was filtered twice and one pot with the figs and a fresh new water. Continue to boil the content of both pots for a few more hours. Stir occasionally.

Follow this method to test for doneness of the juices in both pots:

Take 1 tablespoon of the cooking juice and place it in a saucer. With a knife make a figure of a plus sign (+) on the juice. If the cross comes together and closes the juice is still running and not ready. It needs more boiling time. If the cross remains open and the juice looks thick, it is done.

All the figs by now are almost consumed. Extract all the remaining juice by mash the figs through the food mill. Combine the juice with the rest of both waters previously boiled.

Let it all cool. Meanwhile prepare the sterilized jars to store the vino cotto.

Fill the jars with this delicious nectar while is still warm. Close the jars hermetically. Store in a cool, shaded area and it will keep for 1 year.

Vino cotto is used on cartellate as a sweetener and in the mix of Sassanelli biscotti. Find the recipe in the book.

Baked Dry Figs
Duration: 10 min.

Ingredients for 4 people

1 pack of dried figs

1 small pack of chocolate chips

1 small pack of almonds

a few bay leaves

Preheat oven at 275° F. Take as many dried figs as you like, at least 3 per person.

Split them in half; place one almond in the centre of each fig and some chocolate chips, or chocolate shavings. Close the two halves.

Arrange all the stuffed figs in a clay-baking dish with a few bay leaves placed in the pan and bake them only until the chocolate is melted and the figs are warm. It will take about five to seven minutes. Let them cool down before serving, or storing.

Voila' the simplest dessert you have ever prepared.

These baked figs can be kept in a pretty decorative jar for quite some time and they can be eaten for breakfast, lunch, dinner and any time in between.

If you like, before serving, arrange them in a pretty plate and dust some powdered sugar all over.

Wine: A sparkling Prosecco, or a dessert wine like Marsala will marry nicely with baked figs.

—w—

Drunken Fruit
Duration: 15 min.

Ingredients for 4 people

2 large grapefruits

2 glasses of Muscat, or Sherry,
  or any sweet white wine

1 can of cherries in syrup

4 spoons of sugar

Cut the grapefruits in half and remove the pulp, making sure not to puncture or destroy the peels, they are needed as cups later. Remove the white skin from the pulp as much as possible. Place all the pulp in a bowl; add the cherries without the syrup, sugar and the sweet wine. Keep the mixture in the refrigerator for about two hours, and then fill up each half of the grapefruit peels.

As alternative to the grapefruit skin cups, use martini glasses, or wine goblets as containers for this nice dessert.

Drowned Oranges
Duration: 20 min.

Ingredients for 4 people

4 oranges
2 or 3 oz. of dates
2 or 3 oz. of raw almonds

4 or 5 tablespoons of brown sugar
juice of ½ lemon
½ glass of Grand Marnier, or Cointreau, or Rum

Bring water to a boil in a small pot. Immerge the almonds for only a few seconds to loosen the skin. Pat them dry. Place on a cookie sheet at medium heat to toast them briefly. Chop coarsely.

Peel the oranges and eliminate the bitter white skin too, separate each slice and cut in half. Place them in a glass bowl; add lemon juice, sugar and Grand Marnier, or one of the other liqueurs mentioned in the ingredients.

Chill it for a while, then serve the orange slices with its juice in a glass, add dates and chopped almonds.

For a richer dessert, add an orange sorbet at the bottom of the glass, then the drowned oranges, dates and almonds on top.

—∞—

Mango Flambé With Ice Cream
Duration: 15 min.

Ingredients for 4 people

fresh mangoes as many as you like
a hand full of macadamia nuts
1 cup of brown sugar

2 dollops of butter
Grand Marnier or Brandy
ice cream of your liking

Peel the mangoes and cut them in cubes or slices.

Toast the macadamia nuts and chop them coarsely. Set aside.

In a frying pan, melt 2 dollops of butter, add the brown sugar, stir quickly, then add the mangoes cubed or sliced, and quickly brown them on high fire. Don't stir much, the mangoes will fall apart.

At this point be very careful with the addition of alcohol into the skillet.

Add a few drops of brandy or Grand Marnier to flambé the mangoes and cook off the alcohol. It is a very creative moment, you will see a pretty picture evolving in front of your eyes. The alcohol will create a bluish flame that will give a high dimension to the mangoes. Not to worry, but be attentive, the flame will cook down very quickly. Place hot mangoes in each plate; add toasted macadamia on top and the ice cream of your liking.

Fruit Cocktail
Duration: 15 min.

Ingredients for 4 people
a good bunch of mixed fruit
(the quantities are all up to you)
a hand full of unsalted mixed raw dried nuts
fresh squeezed lemon juice
sugar to your taste
liqueurs: Maraschino, or Sherry, or Drambuie, or Calvados
whipped cream, or gelato (any flavour to your liking)
Italian chocolate biscotti, or Amaretti Italian cookies
a few mint leaves
cacao powder
cocktail decorations

Use fruit with different colours, texture and taste, but don't forget apples and bananas, they function as binder.

Example of fruit to use: apples, mangoes, oranges, tangerines, plums, strawberries, any kind of melons, grapes, pineapples, bananas, any berries and any other fruit available.

Peel all the fruit, cut small bites and place them in a large bowl.

On a baking sheet, roast the mixed raw nuts in the oven for about 8-10 minutes, or toast them on top of the stove in a skillet.

As soon as they have cooled down, chop them coarsely with the half moon cutting tool, if you own one, or in the food processor, but be careful not to reduce the nuts into powder.

To the fruit previously chopped add the roasted or toasted nuts, sugar to your taste, the juice of one or two lemons (depending on the quantity of fruit used) and the liqueur of your liking. Make it very happy.

If kids will eat this fruit cocktail omit the liqueur. Fill large glass wine goblets, or glass bowls with the fruit mixture.

Top it with whipped cream, or gelato to your taste.

In the centre of the fruit cocktail add one or three Italian biscotti (odd numbers look good), or Amaretti cookies.

Sprinkle some mint leaves finely chopped.

Dust with cacao powder and decorate with some cocktail items.

Wine: Bellini chilled, or Italian Spumante.

Strawberry Egg Cream
Duration: 45 min.

Ingredients for 4 people
2 eggs
1.7 oz. of sugar
1 tablespoon of cake flour
vanilla extract to your liking
12.5 oz. of milk
1 or 2 baskets of strawberries
1 teaspoon of powdered sugar
a few mint leaves
1 chocolate biscotto per person

Preheat the oven at 350° F.

Combine eggs and sugar and whisk well. Add one tablespoon of cake flour, vanilla extract to your liking and milk.

Wash and drain the strawberries, cut them lengthwise.

Butter the baking pan you are going to use. Fill it with strawberries first and then with the rest of the ingredients.

Place the baking pan onto a larger baking pan with water for a Bain Marie and allow the eggs to cook thoroughly. Bake until the eggs are coagulated, about 30 minutes.

Dust with powdered sugar when the egg cream is totally cooled, otherwise the powdered sugar will melt, decorate with mint leaves and show it to your guests before serving it.

Serve a large spoon per person with one chocolate biscotto on the side.

Note: Remember Italian sweet are never very sweet, add more sugar if your taste buds requires it.

Wine: Prosecco is always appropriate with any Italian sweet, or a classic champagne.

Three Berries Dessert
Duration: 30 min.

Ingredients for 4 people
1 pre-made pound cake
blue berries, raspberries, strawberries and kumquats in any amount
1 cup of orange juice
1 cup of sugar
Grand Marnier or any liqueur of your liking
1 or 2 biscotti per person
a few leaves of fresh mint

This dessert is so simple and healthy!

The quantity of the ingredients is totally up to your taste. If you like it sweet add more sugar, if you like it thick do not add too much liquids and so on.

In a baking pan, possibly glass, combine blue berries, raspberries, strawberries and kumquats all thinly sliced. If kumquats are not available in your area, use oranges, or tangerines cut in bite sizes.

Add a cup of orange juice, a cup of sugar, and a flavoured liqueur, such as Millefiori, Cointreau, or Grand Marnier.

Bake at 325°F. until thickened, about 15-20 minutes.

Serve it at room temperature in a Martini glass, or in a pretty glass bowl to show the jewel tone colour.

Line the bottom of a Martini glass with broken pieces of pound cake; place on top the baked berries and the juice created during the baking. Decorate it with a hand full of fresh mint leaves, or edible flowers like nasturtium, finish the decoration with one or two biscotti in the centre.

The serving quantity for each person depends on the size of the glass used.

If there is some left over, it can be kept in a glass jar and in the refrigerator up to a week. It will make a nice addition to an ice cream bowl.

Wine: Well chilled Prosecco, a sparkling wine from Veneto, a northern Italian region.

Zabaglione Cream
Duration: 20 min.

Ingredients for 4 people

4 egg yokes

4 tablespoons of brown sugar

8 tablespoons of Marsala liqueur

sweet cacao to your taste

chocolate covered biscotti

a few strawberries

Wash and cut each strawberry in four slices the long way. Set aside.

Combine eggs and sugar in a copper bowl. Wisk vigorously for about 5 minutes. Electric eggbeater is also fine to use. Transfer the bowl on a double boiler, over a medium-low heat. Add Marsala liqueur.

Continue to whisk until the ingredients have become a velvety cream. Be careful not to let it boil, otherwise will turn lumpy. Take the zabaglione cream off the fire. Serve it in an attractive glass, goblet, or cup. Sprinkle cacao powder over the zabaglione.

Add one chocolate covered biscotto inside the glass.

Decorate by inserting four slices of strawberries around the edge of the glass.

Serve semi-warm, or room temperature.

Wine: Well chilled Prosecco, a sparkling Italian wine, from the northern Italian region of Veneto.

—ᴍ—

Ladyfingers and Hazelnuts Cake
Duration: 30 min.

Ingredients for 4 people

1 pack of lady fingers

7 or 8 oz. of brown sugar

a big dollop of butter

6 egg yokes

1 orange

1 teaspoon of powder cinnamon

3 or 4 oz. of hazelnuts

3 or 4 oz. of dark unsweetened chocolate

4-1/2 cup of milk

Butter a baking pan and line it with ladyfingers. Chop hazelnuts and chocolate, set aside.

In another bowl beat the egg yokes separated from the whites, add sugar and beat until a foamy cream has formed (use the white of the eggs to make a different dish later, like a frittata).

Mix in the milk, slowly a bit at a time and stir well.

Pour the mixture onto the ladyfingers and add chopped chocolate.

Place the baking dish into the oven for about 20-25 minutes. Cool it for a while.

Spoon the soft cake in an elegant dish and cover it with roughly chopped hazelnuts.

It can be served warm, or room temperature.

Yogurt And Bananas Sorbet

Duration: 15 min. preparation
1 hr. in the freezer

Ingredients for 4 people

3 bananas not totally ripe
6 spoons of natural yogurt without added flavour
5 tablespoons of sugar
2 tablespoons of Grand Marnier, or any aromatic liqueur
1 or 2 baskets of strawberries
½ cup of sugar, or 5 oz. of sugar, depending on how sweet you like the strawberry cream
a few leaves of fresh mint
candied fruit
a hand full of crushed nuts

Peel and slice the bananas a bit thick. Place the banana slices in a container with a lid and in the freezer to let them get cold for about one hour.

Transfer the bananas into a food processor; add sugar and yogurt to make a dense cream.

Transfer this cream into a container with a lid and place it in the freezer for another hour.

Now make a cream with the strawberries. Wash and put them in the food processor. Add ½ cup of sugar (add more sugar if you want the cream sweeter) and Grand Marnier. Make a puree.

Arrange in the centre plate two spoons of strawberry cream, on top place a couple of balls of the yogurt-bananas sorbet. Decorate the centre of each ball with a few mint leaves, candied fruit and spread all around a hand full of crushed nuts.

Don't keep the sorbet in the freezer for more than an hour. It must be served soft, not frozen, otherwise it will loose the delicate taste It must be consumed all at once, it does not keep well.

Two Summer Delights

Lemon Verbena Sorbet
Duration: 15 min. to prepare
4 or 5 hrs. in the freezer

This recipe doesn't need a list of ingredients.

Use 1 cup of water per person, sugar to your liking, and 1 bunch of lemon verbena per person. Blend everything and strain. Add more sugar, if you want it sweeter.

Transfer into a baking pan, or Pyrex pan, place it in the freezer and stir every 20 minutes to form a kind of ice grenadine mixture. After about 4 to 5 hours will be ready to serve into chilled glasses.

To make it into ice cream, place the mixture in single ice cream containers, add ice cream sticks inside each one and freeze it.

—∞—

Orange Sorbet
Duration: 20 min. to prepare
4 or 5 hrs. in the freezer

Peel about 10 oranges, keep away the white spongy part and chop all the rinds.

Fill a saucepan with water, add all the orange rinds, sugar to your liking, or let's say about 2 tablespoons of sugar per person and bring it to a boil.

Add more sugar if you like the mixture sweeter.

Transfer into a baking pan, place it in the freezer and stir every 20 minutes to form a kind of ice grenadine mixture. After about 4 to 5 hours will be ready to serve into chilled glasses.

To make it into ice cream, place the mixture in single ice cream containers, add ice cream sticks inside each one and freeze it.

Candied Orange Rinds
Duration: 4 days drying time

Ingredients
7 oz. of orange rinds
5.2 oz. of sugar

Peel oranges very close to the skin, stay away from the white part of the skin, it is spongy and bitter. Julienne cut all the peels, place them in a stainless steel pan (not aluminium), add sugar and enough water to cover them only above the top. Slowly boil for about ten minutes. Let the peel rest in that water for 24 hours, then take them out with a fork an put them to rest spread out in a plate.

Second day, boil again the syrupy water of the orange rinds for about five minute. Return the orange rinds again in the syrupy boiling water for five more minutes.

Turn off the fire and let them rest for another 24 hours. This time don't take the orange rinds out of the syrup.

Third day, return the syrupy water and the orange rinds to the fire again, bring it to a brief boil, five minutes.

Pick up the orange rinds with a fork and set them to dry on a plate well divided from each other for additional 24 hours. On the fourth day, the orange rinds will be just about dried, roll them in additional sugar over and over to coat them well. Leave to dry.

When they are well dried, conserve them in a decorative glass jar, inside or outside the refrigerator. This specialty keeps for a long time.

Special Uses
Eat them any time alone, or with nuts, or mixed in with salads.

Use candied orange rinds when making any cake mixed in with ingredients.

Add them to any roast or game meat.

Use them in place of sugar when serving coffee, tea and cookies.

They can be covered with dark chocolate sauce and in this case, place them in the refrigerator to harden before serving.

Candied orange rinds are a good boost of energy, but they are not very sweet.

Lemon peel can be done the same way.

Candied Edible Flower Petals
Some edible flowers are: calendula also called marigold, nasturtium, day lilies and carnations; violets, pansies, rose petals and lilac; borage, pea, pinks scented geraniums.

Beat one egg white until foamy, add one teaspoon of water to spread the egg white easier. With a small paintbrush paint each flower petal on all sides. Sprinkle granulated sugar on each one and all over. Align the petals on wax paper to dry. They will get hard and will be ready to be placed on a cake, or as accompaniment to tea and biscotti, or to decorate a cheese display.

Note: You should NEVER use pesticides or other chemicals on any part of any plant that produces blossoms you plan on eating. Never harvest flowers growing by the roadside to turn into candied flowers.

Pears Gratinée
Duration: 40 min.

Ingredients for 4 people
4 pears
3 or 4 oz. of day old Italian bread,
or left over sponge cake
2 tablespoons of butter
¼ cup of brown sugar
1 cup of walnuts, or almonds, or hazelnuts
dark semi-sweet chocolate
1 scoop of ice cream (any flavour) or whipped cream

Slice the pears about ¼" thick. In a gratin dish arrange one pear overlapping the other until all the pear slices are used up.

In a food processor, crumble the bread, or the sponge cake coarsely.

Add butter, sugar and nuts. Process it until the mixture looks like a corn meal.

Spread it over the pears evenly.

Bake in a preheated oven at 375°F for about 30 minutes until the top is golden brown.

Let it cool down at room temperature, then serve it with or without ice cream, or whipped cream.

Shave some dark chocolate and sprinkle it over, before serving.

—∞—

Bananas Gratinée
Duration: 15 min.

Ingredients for 4 people
5 or 6 bananas
juice of 1 lemon
a hand full of raisins

¼ cup brown sugar
½ cup Cointreau or Rum

Peel five or six bananas. Place them in a gratin pan.

Flavour the bananas with either liqueur.

Sprinkle brown sugar and add the juice of a small lemon over them.

Place under the broil for few minutes, or until golden brown.

Garnish with the peel of a lemon finely grated and a sprinkle of raisins.

Serve warm.

Torte of Caramelized Peaches
Duration: 35 min.

Ingredients for 4 people

pre-made pound cake

4 or 5 peaches

brown sugar to your taste

cookies of your liking such as:

amaretti, cantuccini, butter cookies, chocolate cookies.

whipped cream

orange peels

1 stick of butter

Peel all the peaches, cut in small cubes, and place them in a skillet with brown sugar.

Cook until lightly caramelized. Grate the peel of one orange and add it to the peaches.

Cut the pound cake in round disks, each about ½" thick to fit into each ramekin and butter both sides of the disks. Butter each ramekin and fill them up in layers: one disk of pound cake, a layer of caramelized peaches and one pound cake disk. If the ramekin is large, continue in the same fashion, until the top is reached.

Place all the ramekins on a baking sheet and bake for about 15 minutes at 375° F. Then place them under the broiler to golden the tops. To serve, slip a knife around the walls to loosen the content, turn over each ramekin on a plate, remove the torte and cover the top with whipped cream. Crumble some cookies of your liking as a final decoration, or arrange them on one side of the torte.

Wine: Prosecco, an Italian sparkling wine from the northern region of Veneto.

—m—

Melon Mix With Mint and Dried Figs
Duration: 20 min.

Ingredients for 4 people

1 cantaloupe melon, 1 honeydew melon

2 spoons of brown sugar

a hand full of mint chopped

black pepper to taste

a hand full of dried figs

a hand full of dried walnuts

1 or 2 cups of sugar

honey

Peel and deseed the melons, chop them in bite sizes.

In a bowl mix melons, grated ginger, sugar and black pepper. Mix well and let it rest for a while, it will create its own juice. Cut the figs in half, place one walnut inside, close the fig and roll it in sugar and then in honey. Place them on a non-stick baking sheet, or grease the baking sheet and place under the broiler until caramelized. Serve them together with the melon mix.

Celebration of carnevale in Putignano

Putignano is a small ancient town in the South of Italy in the region of Puglia built between hills at about 18 Km from the Adriatic Sea.

The original ancient borough was made in the elliptical shape surrounded by tall walls to protect the town from foreign invaders. Through the centuries those walls have fallen and left a great hole in place.

For over seven centuries Putignano was a protectorate of the Pope and for about two centuries the town was under the dependence of the Knights of Malta, a very powerful religious organization.

Its inhabitants were always into agriculture work, which produced the renowned healthy Puglia country food. In addition people of Putignano produced quality hand-made crafts like cotton and felt creations and the most exquisites internationally known wedding gowns. In the last fifty years Putignano became known for its Carnival floats also famous all over the world. The Carnevale of Putignano starts on December 26th with the celebration of "**Propaggine**" and it is over on Mardi Gras day of the following year.

The Propaggine (offshoot) is an ancient method used to grow grapevine. The branch of the grapevine is curved in a "U shape" and imbedded into a fresh ground without cutting it from the main plant. Before putting the branch under the ground, a small part of the skin of the branch at the base of the "U shape" is cut off to allow a new root to find its way out. One leg of the "U shape" curved branch is still attached to the main plant, the base of the "U shape" goes under the ground and the other leg of the "U shape" is then attached to a pole. After a while a new root will form and the curved branch can be cut off from the main plant to have its own life. The part attached to the pole will be the new vine. This method is also used to grow precious plants.

The celebration of the Propaggine goes back to December 26, 1394.

It was a day the remaining of St. Stephen were transported from the Monastery in Monopoli, Puglia to the Abbey in Putignano, Puglia where they are still kept today.

At the passage of St. Stephen's remaining, the farmers who were attending the grapevines, left the fields to follow the saint in a cortege, improvising a happy celebration with songs and dances and the Propaggine celebration was born, so the legend says. This is a feast, which started with lot of religious connotations, still celebrated every December 26th, but today the Propaggine has acquired a satirical flavor. It is an opportunity to mock political figures in the world, along with prominent people of the town. Nobody is excluded from the satire and jokes: priest, nuns, monsignors, singles, widowers, married women and everybody that has been in the news during the year. The celebration brings the community together during the whole year while preparing the floats, which go on parade the day of Mardi Gras.

The symbolic costume of Carnevale in Putignano is "Farinella".

The name of Farinella comes from an ancient farmer's dish made of chickpeas flour and roasted barley that gets mixed with sauces or it accompanies fresh figs. Flour in Italian translates in farina, thus farinella means light flour.

The costume even though takes origins from an ancient dish, is really a fairly new creation, invented in 1953 and it almost looks like Pulcinella costume.

The figure represents a happy joker dressed in a patched up costume of many colors, it has a blue collar around the neck, hat and shoes with small bells attached. It looks good on kids.

Carnevale ends on the Mardi Gras day with the parade of colorful floats more than twenty-two feet tall, hand made by skillful local artisans, followed by the symbolic funeral of Carnevale represented as a pig.

The typical cookies prepared for this event is called Chiacchiere, meaning chitchat, friable cookies. They are made in large quantities for a large crowd of friends. Chiacchiere cookies are like cherries, one pulls the other. Find the recipe on the next page.

"People who laugh live longer. People who love age slower,
run faster, jump higher, eat healthier,
are as happy with friends as they are alone
and take off on Fridays "
♥

Colorful Floats Of Carnevale In Putignano, Italy

Chiacchiere
(Chitchat Cookies)
Duration: 40 min.

Ingredients for 4 to 6 people
17.5 oz. of white flour
4 whole eggs
1.7 oz. of butter
1.5 oz. of brown sugar
4 tablespoons of Cointreau, or Grand Marnier, or Rum
canola or vegetable oil to fry (no peanut, nor palm oil)
powdered sugar

Mix all the ingredients well. Make a soft ball. Let it rest for about 1/2 hour.

Cut the dough ball into many pieces of 2-½" long x ½" wide. Twist each piece like a rope.

In a skillet warm up the vegetable oil, drop each piece slowly and fry them until they are all gone.

Drain the excess oil on an absorbent paper.

Let them cool down on a rack, dust powdered sugar on it.

Legend
These cookies are very crunchy. It is believed the noise these cookies produce when people eat them is similar to the noise women produce when they are together chatting and gossiping.

Sassanelli Biscotti
Duration: 45 min.

Ingredients for 4 to 6 people

17.5 oz. of toasted almonds

35 oz. of flour

8.5 oz. of sugar

5.2 oz. of olive oil or butter

0.4 oz. of baking powder

1 cup of Vincotto[1]

cinnamon to your taste

cloves to your taste and chopped

vanilla to your taste

First toast the almonds in the oven for about 8-10 minutes, watch them carefully they easily burn. Chop them medium fine.

The mixing can be done with the food processor by adding all the ingredients together at once. If mixing by hands, put down the flour on a flat surface, make a well in the centre and place all the ingredients inside. Mix all to form a ball of a medium hard consistency.

Form small balls of 3" in diameter. Align them on a baking sheet and bake at 355° F. for about 18 minutes. While cooling they will keep firming up, then Sassanelli can be stored in a cookie jar.

What is Vincotto?

Vincotto is a cooked wine must of Negroamaro and black Malvasia grapes cultivated in the South of Italy.

The wine must is aged in oak barrels for a long time.

Vincotto is a versatile ingredient that goes beyond dressing salads. It is used as condiment over roasted meats (only a few drops are needed), over vegetables and drizzled over chunks of Parmigiano cheese to be served at the end of a dinner. It also blends well with bacon and roasted potatoes. It mixes nicely in some sweets and desserts of Puglia, adding an interesting zest. Vinocotto is also made with fresh figs as in the Cartellate recipe in this book.

Cultural Note

Sassanelli is the Italian word for little pebbles. Up until the last century in the Region of Puglia, Sassanelli were given to children in a burlap sack as the only Christmas gift.

Kids visited the homes of their relatives to get as many sweets as possible. If they had been bad during the year they would find real pebbles in their sacks, but if they had been good they would be rewarded with Sassanelli.

The tradition has remained and every Christmas Sassanelli are baked in every home of Puglia and can even be found in the best Pastry shoppes. Each biscotto could weights 0.4 oz. During holidays Sassanelli are sold in very attractive bags containing ten biscotti each.

Zeppole

(Soft Doughnuts)

Duration: 60 min.

Ingredients for 4 to 6 people

4.4 oz. of flour	4 egg yokes	8.5 fluid oz. of water
1 tablespoon of sugar	3.5 oz. of butter	a pinch of salt
a pinch of baking powder	grated peel of 1 lemon or 1 orange	
1 teaspoon of cinnamon	vegetable oil or corn oil to fry	
cherry or strawberry marmalade	(no peanut oil nor palm oil)	

In a pot bring 8.5 fluid oz. of water to a boil with the butter, sugar and a pinch of salt.

Pour all the flour in the water at once and stir briskly until a ball has formed and comes away from the pan. Turn the fire off and cool down the ball. Transfer the ball into a bowl; incorporate the rest of the ingredients and egg yokes one by one. Beat and whip well until the ball has become a yellow sticky dough. Place the sticky dough inside a pastry pouch with a tip that will produce ridges when the dough goes through. Lay down a large piece of parchment paper.

Squeeze the mixture in the pouch onto the parchment paper to form as many doughnuts (without a hole in the centre) of about 3" in diameter. Before frying, cut the parchment paper in many squares around each dough to help managing the sticky dough. In a frying pan warm up the oil, hold each doughnut by the paper and drop it in the hot oil. When one side is firm enough, the paper will not stick any more and will come off easy from the top, then turn the doughnut over and fry the other side. After they are cooled down, place a dollop of marmalade on one side of the doughnut to add colour. One good variation is to fill the inside with a pastry cream. Zeppole can be baked. They are healthier, but less friable.

—⁂—

Pastry Cream

Ingredients for 4 to 6 people

4.2 cups of milk	grated lemon peel	4.4 oz. of flour
1 or 2 teaspoons of vanilla	2.8 oz. of sugar	4 whole eggs

Place all the ingredients in a saucepan. At a very slow fire cook by stirring constantly until a smooth, silky cream has formed. Fill up a pastry pouch with this mixture and then stuff zeppole.

Legend

Every year on March 19th Italy celebrates St. Joseph, Jesus Christ's father and the patron of all carpenters, because he was a carpenter himself. In the piazzas of most towns in Italy, many bonfires are built for burning wood, old chairs and tables, old furniture and anything in wood. The bonfires are made in St. Joseph's honour and also to kick away bad spirits and bad luck. Good things and good luck will be welcomed after the bonfire has quieted down. Then zeppole are passed around to celebrate.

Zeppole

Candied Almonds
Duration: 80 min.

Ingredients for 4 to 6 people
3 cups of shelled almonds
cinnamon to your liking
1 cup of sugar
a small pinch of salt
2 tablespoons of dry white wine
2 egg whites beaten

Mix all the ingredients well. Bake at 250° F for about 1 hour, stirring every 20 minutes. Keep them separated.

Let them cool. Store the candied almonds in a pretty container. Decorate the container with raffia, ribbons, or anything that pleases your eyes.

Candied almonds will keep for a few months.

Serve them with coffee, or as accompaniment to a fruit plate, or to ice cream.

Keep them handy to munch on when you have a desire.

—∞—

Torroncini
Duration: 25 min.

Ingredients for 4 to 6 people
8.8 oz. of flour
10.5 oz. of sugar
8.8 oz. of toasted almonds
grated peels of 1 orange and 1 lemon
1 tablespoon of vanilla

3.5 oz. of unsweetened cacao
1 teaspoon of cinnamon
2 or 3 grinded cloves
1 cup of sweet white wine

Place the flour on a flat surface, add all the ingredients.
Mix well making sure the dough comes out sufficiently hard.
Cut the dough in many rectangular pieces, shape and cut them in a diagonal way.
Butter and flour a cookie sheet, place all the cut pieces at 2″ apart.
Bake for about ten minutes at a medium temperature, about 375° F.

The legend of Torrone

Torrone is a typical Italian Christmas delicacy made in the town of Cremona, in the North of Italy. Some people consider it a candy bar, but in reality it is one of the many sweets produced in large quantities through the Christmas holidays.

Its principal ingredients are eggs, toasted almonds, hazelnuts and vanilla.

Torrone is made in a soft or hard bar, white or dark with chocolate base.

The legend says that in 1441 a special sweet made of almonds, honey and egg whites was prepared for the wedding between Francesco Sforza and Bianca Maria Visconti.

The sweet creation was made in the shape of the cathedral's bell tower of Cremona, the renowned "Torrazzo" shooting up in the air 369 feet.

This seems to be not a true story, but it was instead an ingenious marketing strategy, a story made up by the company, which invented Torrone.

Torrone's feast in Cremona starts at the end on November in the centre town and marks the opening of Christmas holidays. There are a blaze of kiosks, Torrone tasting areas, historical re-enactments and games, along with the feast for kids, during which children can visit certain city routes defined for them and learn about history, architecture in the simple way, costumes and customs of the era.

Almond Rocks
Duration: 20 min.

There is no measuring of ingredients for this recipe; the quantity is up to you.

Try first 2 cups of slivered almonds, 1-1/2 cup of sugar and 1-1/2 cup of chopped chocolate pieces. Increase or decrease the measurements, as you like.

Spread all the slivered almonds on a wax paper.

In a small saucepan melt the sugar at low heat to make a caramel. Keep stirring the sugar until it gets golden/brown in colour. It will burn easily if you don't stir constantly.

Cover the almonds with the caramel, mix well with a fork and let it cool.

Melt the chocolate pieces in a double boiler over a low fire, by stirring constantly to avoid burning and sticking the chocolate to the pan.

Pour the melted chocolate over the almonds, again mix well and let it cool for about 15-20 minutes.

Wait until the almonds are totally cooled down to break them into irregular pieces looking like small rocks.

It makes a good gift for the holidays.

—⁓—

Macadamia Brittles
Duration: 20 min.

Again there are no measurements for this recipe, the quantity of the ingredients are up to you.

Place a wax paper on a baking sheet and all the macadamia on top, let's say 2 cups. Toast them for about 10 minutes at 350° F.

In a double boiler melt chocolate chips or chunks of dark chocolate into a silky, smooth cream. Pour it over the toasted macadamia. Allow 15-20 minutes to harden, then cut uneven shapes.

This also makes a good gift for the holidays, especially when you create a medley of baked, toasted, caramelized nuts, candied orange peels, candied edible flower petals and cookies or biscotti. What a treat for those who receive it.

Almond Rocks

Castagnelle Biscotti
Duration: 45 min.

Ingredients for 6 to 8 people
17.5 oz. of almonds
17.5 oz. of sugar
17.5 oz. of flour
3 whole eggs
3.5 oz. of unsweetened cacao
some kind of sweet liquor, Sherry or Cointreau
1.2 oz. of baking powder
grated peel of 1 orange
chopped dark chocolate to your taste
2 teaspoons of vanilla
1 teaspoon of cinnamon
enough water to mix all the ingredients

Toast the almonds for about 10 minutes in the oven; chop them coarsely.

The quantity of chopped dark chocolate is totally up to your taste.

Mix all the ingredients by gradually adding water until a compact, but elastic dough is formed.

Form small balls of about 2.5" in diameter. Preheat oven at 355° F.

Lightly oil and flour a baking sheet and align all the balls, but leave a space in between each other to allow them to grow in the baking process.

Bake for about 15-18 minutes, castagnelle biscotti must be soft.

While cooling they will keep firming up, then castagnelle can be stored in a cookie jar.

Raisins Biscotti
Duration: 40 min.

Ingredients for 4 to 6 people

1 cup of all purpose flour	1 egg and 1 egg yoke
1 cup of yellow corn meal	a few drops of vanilla extract
1/3 cup of sugar	grated lemon peel
¼ teaspoon of salt	black currants or dry raisins
1 teaspoon of baking powder	1 stick of butter

On a flat surface, mix all the dry ingredients first reducing them into breadcrumbs consistency. Use a fork to mix, or better the hand held Pastry Blender. This device has six sturdy blades and an oversized handle for superior performance when blending butter or shortening into dry ingredients.

Add the rest of the ingredients and whisk well, including the currants or raisins.

Make dough the same way as for any biscotti. After a ball is formed, roll the dough into a thick tube, about 2" wide. At this point, proceed in either of the two ways, whichever would be most convenient to you:

Bake the roll of dough for 20 minutes at 350° F. When it comes out of the oven, cool it briefly, then cut diagonal pieces of about 1-1/2" thickness, place them on a cookie sheet and bake them again for 10-12 more minutes at 350° F.

OR

Cut the raw dough into small pieces about 1-1/2" wide, place them on a cookie sheet and bake at 350° F. for about 20 minutes. This second way will produce a softer texture.

Anise Biscotti
Duration: 30 min.

Ingredients for 4 to 6 people
3 cups of all-purpose flour
1 teaspoon of baking powder
¼ teaspoon of salt
2 teaspoons of anise seeds or Pernod liqueur
1-1/2 stick of unsalted butter
1 cup of sugar
2 whole eggs
1-1/2 teaspoon of vanilla

Preheat oven at 350˚ F.

Mix all the dry ingredients to breadcrumbs consistency. Use a fork to mix, or better the hand held Pastry Blender. This device has six sturdy blades and an oversized handle for superior performance when blending butter or margarine into dry ingredients.

Incorporate the wet ingredients and work them into a ball. Keep the dough ball in the refrigerator for half hour to harden it.

Cut ½" slices one at a time and keep the rest covered under a plastic wrap to keep it moist.

Cut each slice in half. Roll out each slice into 4" long round tubes of about ¼ " diameter.

Bend each tube in a ribbon shape; twist the ends as if making a knot.

Bake about 18-20 minutes until crunchy. Check them often, they are easy to burn.

Anise Biscotti

Suggested Italian wines to combine with sweets

Caluso Passito D.O.C. – *from the region of Piemonte.*
Its production evolves around Torino, Biella and Vercelli, but especially around Caluso, which is the center of the Canavese area. The first phase of the production is the withering of the grapes onto mats, or wooden crates and it is the most important phase. The grapes are divided from one another to dry them uniformly to assure a good quality wine.
Colour: *from light golden yellow to dark amber*
Bouquet: *delicate*
Taste: *sweet, mellow*

Cartizze Spumante D.O.C. – *from the region of Veneto.*
It is cultivated in the province of Treviso, around Valdobbiadene and Conegliano. The fermentation happens with selected yeasts in controlled temperature areas, the foam is created in heavy vessels and at low temperature.
Colour: *light golden yellow with greenish highlight*
Bouquet: *fruity, delicate*
Taste: *dry with slightly sweet aftertaste*

Malvasia Nera di Brindisi D.O.C. and **D.O.C.G.** – *from the region of Puglia in the Salento area.*
It is mostly a Mediterranean grape, originally generated in Greece and Aegean islands. The origin of the name Malvasia comes from a fine, high quality wine the Venetian people commercialized before the 800 B.C. The Malvasia produced today includes all the Muscats with a light aroma and fruity types made with dark and light grapes.
Colour: *from red cherry to ruby red*
Bouquet: *aromatic*
Taste: *roasted walnut, sweet*

Moscato di Trani D.O.C. – *from the region of Puglia.*
It is cultivated in Trani and surrounding areas. It is obtained by leaving the grapes to mature almost to a withering point. The area of Trani produces the sweet Moscato and the liqueur Moscato, which is aged for one year and it has higher alcohol content. Both must be served in dessert glasses and at a temperature between 50-53° F.
Colour: *amber yellow*
Bouquet: *sweet, dry roses*
Taste: *full body, aromatic*

Greco di Gerace D.O.C. - *from the region of Calabria.*
Its origins go back to ancient Greece. The wine is made from Greco white or red grapes grown on the seaside of Calabria and it is often blended with Malvasia grapes. The white Greco grape tend to mature late in the grapevine season, therefore is easy to find mildew on the vine.
Colour: *yellow amber*
Bouquet: *aromatic, typical of raisins*
Taste: *mellow*

Suggested Italian wines to combine with sweets
Continue

Giro' di Cagliari D.O.C. - *from the island of Sardegna.*

The vine originated in Spain around the 18th century. Marquis di Rivarolo a Piedmontese ruling the island brought it to the island of Sardegna. Today this vine grows on the calcareous soil around Cagliari province.

Colour: *brilliant ruby red*
Bouquet: *delicate, dry, elegant*
Taste: *sweet like a liqueur, viscous*

Mamertino D.O.C. - *from the island of Sicily.*

It is considered one of the fine wines of the area. Its grape was planted around 289 B.C. at the bottom of the Etna Volcano long before the Phoenician merchants touched the islands. It is made of Nero D'Avola grapes and Nocera grapes, aged for one year, six months of which are spent aging in wood barrels.

Colour: *golden yellow*
Bouquet: *delicate*
Taste: *sweet, smooth*

Vin Santo D.O.C. – *from the region of Tuscany.*

It is made of Trebbiano and Malvasia grapes. One of the many legend of this wine talks about a Franciscan monk from Siena. In 1348 the monk cured people afflicted with the bubonic plague by letting them drink this wine. The wine was considered miraculous, thus the origin of the name Santo. It is made of a blend of white grapes, specifically Trebbiano Toscano and Malvasia, with an occasional mix of Grechetto.

Colour: *golden yellow or amber*
Bouquet: *accentuated due to high sugar concentration*
Taste: *Viscous*

Why Italians place an initial next to the wine's name?

New laws and regulations from the E.U. (European Union) have made impossible for other countries outside the E.U. to emulate, copy or counterfeit food products made in Italy and in Europe. The same is valid for any other product or merchandise made by the fashion industries, but the initials are different than food products.

There are many initials next to the name of wines, I will report only the main three mostly used:

D.O.C. - Denominazione di Origine Controllata. It means that in order for the wine to be authentic its origin must be controlled.

D.O.C.G. - Denominazione di Origine Controllata e Garantita. It means that in order for the wine to be authentic its origin must be controlled and guaranteed.

I.G.T. - Indicazione Geografica Tipica. It is only used to indicate large production areas for wines made in large quantities. Name of vines and colour of wines produced must also appear next to these initials.

Special Glasses For Your Drinks

Glass to use with all sweet wines and wines made with withered grapes

Plain glass, fine crystal is better, small chalice, slightly bombe' and stocky with a smaller mouth. This shape allows the unfolding of all the aromas in the glass and all their concentration in the nose.

Glass to use with all liqueur-type wines

It is a small glass, slightly taller than the glass used for sweet wines with a larger mouth. The larger opening allows the wine to rest on the tip of the tongue, which is the part of the tongue most sensitive to taste sweetness.

Glass to use with Spumante and sparkling-type wines

Tall and thin flute glass. The long and narrow body allows the development in the mouth of fine "perlage" meaning it allows to taste the thin bubbles or pearls in the young wines produced with the classic method of all sparkling wines.

Flute glass with belly and a larger opening, allows the oxygenation of the sparkling wine and the right development in the mouth of complex aromas found in mature grapes without compromising the savouring of the "perlage".

Half flute glass is shorter than the flute. It is made to taste dry Spumante type of wines with a less refined "perlage" and larger bubbles. The tight opening allows a good concentration of the delicate aromas towards the nose and a slow development of carbon dioxide.

Limoncello
(Lemon Cordial Drink)
Duration: 10 min. preparation
30 days to macerate

Ingredients for ¼ gallon
8 lemons
34 fluid oz. of alcohol at 95° proof or Vodka
21 oz. of sugar
17 fluid oz. of plain water

Limoncello is one of the easiest liquors to make with only a few ingredients and like most Italian recipes, it varies from region to region.

Peel the lemons away from the white skin, which is spongy and bitter.

Place all the lemon rinds in a glass jar, possibly with a cap that closes hermetically and seals well with a rubber gasket. Pour in the 95° proof alcohol.

Close the jar well and leave the lemon rinds to macerate in the alcohol for thirty days in a dark place, a cupboard or a pantry. After this time filter the content.

The lemon juice extracted from the lemon rinds will be poured into a clear glass bottle, better if it is a decorative bottle.

In a small pan mix 21 oz. of sugar and 17 fluid oz. of water, on a low-medium fire to melt the sugar until is totally dissolved into a simple syrup.

Let it cool down and add it to the macerated lemon juice in the bottle.

Cap the bottle and keep it in the refrigerator to settle for a week, then it will be ready to be drunk.

Always serve limoncello very chilled with very chilled glasses kept in the refrigerator too.

Limoncello is good to drink as an after dinner digestive, or as an accompaniment to a dessert.

Nocino Al Caffe'
(Coffee Flavoured Walnut Liqueur)
Duration: 10 min. preparation
40 days to macerate

Ingredients for ¼ gallon

17 green walnuts
¼ gallon of pure alcohol
10 coffee beans
1 small piece of cinnamon

a few cloves
a few lemon rinds
¼ gallon of dry white wine
28.5 oz. of sugar

Wash the young green walnuts and cut them in four parts the long way.

Place them in a glass jar with the alcohol, 10 coffee beans, cinnamon (use the cinnamon sparingly, otherwise it will overpower the walnuts), a few cloves and lemon rinds.

The green walnuts can be left quartered, or can be crushed in the mortar and pestle.

Leave it to macerate for 40 days in the sun. Stir the content every six or seven days by turning the jar up side down a few times.

This is where the "40 days and 40 nights" nickname for this liqueur comes from.

After the fortieth day is over, filter the walnuts through a cheesecloth, or a tight mesh colander.

In a pot with all the sugar, bring the white wine to a boil. Let it cool down.

In a bottle combine the cooked wine and the filtered walnuts.

Let the mixture age in a dark place, or in a wine cellar for about three months, then it will be ready to be drunk as an after dinner digestive.

Note: Young green walnuts can also be found inside of the apricot pits.

Legend

The young green walnuts must be harvested between the night of the 23rd and 24th of June, day in which St. John is celebrated ever since the year 354 B.C.

St. John was a prophet; he baptized Christ and became his first apostle. His life ended in his own martyrdom, which has been honoured and celebrated ever since in the whole Christian Europe. The Church set the date of his celebration to be six months before the birth of Christ and on the same cadence of the pagan Summer Solstice celebration.

Strangely, as all the strange things that happen on the night of St. John, the Nocino has been tied to the pagan Summer Solstice celebration, even though it is a religious event. Greeks and Romans believed the sun and the moon were married during the Summer Solstice, therefore this day was also dedicated to the celebration of the womanhood, her fertility and marriage. On this day young ladies were allowed to choose some herbs to make love potions with.

I guess Nocino would be considered the love potion of this particular day.

In some areas of Puglia, the region where I come from, Nocino is called Padre Peppe.

It was named after a monk, who invented the formula, which he kept secret for all his life. Before dieing the monk Padre Peppe revealed it to one of the member of the Striccoli family and today the connoisseurs of food can still enjoy it, as it is served everywhere in restaurants of central-south Italy and it is made in most homes.

Chocolate Liqueur
Duration: 10 min.

Ingredients for ¼ gallon
2 cups of milk
12.5 oz. of brown sugar
2.8 oz. of bitter cacao
3.5 fluid oz. of pure alcohol or Vodka
a few Julienne lemon peels

In a saucepan, mix well sugar and cacao, add milk and briefly bring to a boil.
Cool the mixture, and then add the alcohol and the lemon peels.
Fill up a bottle, keep it refrigerated. It is very nice to serve with espresso.

Many thanks to my sister Cristina for this recipe who will be surprised to see it in my book.

—⚉—

Cassis Champagne
Duration: 15 min. preparation
a few hours in the freezer

The mixture will make cassis for 10-12 people.

For this recipe there is no need for a list of ingredients. Only a few baskets of raspberries and blue berries are needed, depending on the number of people you are serving. Let's say 3 or 4 baskets of these two berries together are sufficient to serve six people.

In a saucepan, combine 21 oz. of sugar and 17 fluid oz. of water, on a low-medium fire. Melt the sugar until is totally dissolved into a simple syrup. Add all the berries and cook them down. Cool the mixture.

Line a terrine with plastic wrap long enough to hang over the sides.

Pour in the cooled mixture, let the plastic wrap hang over the sides of the terrine, it will help you later in removing the mixture. Cover the terrine with aluminium foil. Place it in the freezer for a few hours until it has become solid. Take out the cassis, now solid, out of the terrine by pulling the plastic film hanging over the sides and remove the aluminium too.

Cut the solid cassis into 3″ x ½″ long pieces.

Drop each piece of solid berries into fluted Champagne glasses, fill up with Prosecco, a type of Italian sparkling wine or Champagne, as you prefer.

This is refreshing novelty that will surprise your guests.

Conserved Peaches
Duration: 20 min. preparation
2 months of maceration

Ingredients for ¼ gallon

7 or 8 peaches hard and not well ripe
2 cups of plain vinegar
2-1/2 cups of sugar
a few cloves
2 sticks of cinnamon
2 or 3 pieces of candied ginger

Wash the peaches. In a pot bring water to a boil. Drop in the peaches with the skin. Parboil for 1 minute.

Transfer the peaches in a bowl full of water and ice to stop the cooking.

Peel the skin off.

Place a few cloves inside of the flesh of each peach.

Place the peaches in another pot filled with 2 cups of vinegar and bring to a boil at medium fire.

Cook to "fork tender". This means that the peaches are not totally cooked, but fork goes in the flesh easy.

Transfer the warm peaches in a glass jar well sterilized, add the cooking juice, ginger and cinnamon.

Close and seal the jar while it is still warm to create a vacuum.

After 2 months the peaches will be ready for consumption.

It is better to prepare them around August when the fruit is less expensive and it will be ready for Thanksgiving.

Strawberries Liqueur

Strawberries Liqueur
Duration: 10 min. preparation
30 days of maceration
30 days of rest

Ingredients for ¼ gallon
34 fluid oz. of pure alcohol 90° proof or Vodka
17.5 oz. of small strawberries
34 fluid oz. of water
24.5 oz. of sugar

Wash the small strawberries, take out leaves and stems. Manage with care.

Place the strawberries in a glass jar with a lid that closes hermetically, pour in the alcohol and let them macerate for at least 30 days. Gently turn the jar up side down every three days and return it to the up right position.

After this time, make simple syrup with water and sugar. Bring it to a boil and stir constantly with a wooden spoon until the sugar is all melted.

Let it cool before filling the bottle.

Filter the macerated strawberries through a cheesecloth or a tight mesh colander.

With the help of a funnel, transfer the cooled mixture into a decorative glass bottle, shake the bottle gently. Mix in a little more alcohol, if you like it stronger, but I say it is not necessary. Close with a tight cap.

Let it rest for another month, and then it will be ready for consumption.

Many thanks to my friend Gino in Bari for sharing his recipe with me. He makes this liqueur every year and gives it as a gift to his best people.

Life is too short, eat the dessert first.

♥

Also by Valentina Cirasola

Come Mia Nonna

Octavian, a Roman Emperor once said "slow down, we are in a hurry". This book is a tribute to slow food and appreciation of life, a life made with human rhythms.

A return to simplicity because these recipes from the Region of Puglia, in Italy are so very uncomplicated that even if you have never cooked in your life, you will be able to put an attractive dinner together in a short, short time.

Learn more at: www.outskirtspress.com/ComeMiaNonna

LaVergne, TN USA
15 December 2010
208779LV00005B